D1024677

"*The Choice* presents a clear, biblically-grounded framework that challenges and encourages us as believers to focus our calling and lives on kingdom outcomes that make an eternal difference, and to deal head on with the lies of the enemy who tempts us today. All who make the choice to demonstrate that Jesus is in control, Jesus is whom we serve, and Jesus is our core identity will rock this world and bring glory to God. *The Choice* is powerful, purposeful, intentional, pragmatic, and can be a resource to every kingdom leader and their leadership teams and boards. I look forward to a deliberate engagement with my leadership team!"

Larry D. Andrews, President & CEO
Partners International

"Do not start a strategic plan for your board or hold a vision retreat for your leadership team without first reading this book. It will save you from awkward acquiescing and the stress of realigning later on. Hoag, Rodin, and Willmer succinctly describe the path to pleasing God and achieving the right results through our ministries and organizations, and they provide a plethora of practical advice to keep us on that proper course."

John Ashmen, President
Association of Gospel Rescue Missions

"We want to impact the entire world for Jesus. So surely that which is bigger, involves more people and accomplishes more ministry is always better, right? Hoag, Rodin, and Willmer open the Bible and show us what true kingdom principles actually are, guiding both ministry leader and fund-raiser through the maze of competing voices in our world today, including our Christian world. If you want to understand true kingdom stewardship, this little gem of a book is essential reading."

Craig L. Blomberg, PhD, Distinguished Professor
of New Testament, Denver Seminary

"You will find yourself in this book. And unknowingly, you are walking one of two paths. Whether you are sitting in the pew, preaching in the pulpit, practicing spiritual formation, or providing leadership for some missional community, you need this book to keep you on the kingdom path!"

Dave Carder, Counseling Ministries Pastor
First Evangelical Free Church, Fullerton, CA

"Hoag, Rodin, and Willmer understand the gospel pattern: daily faithfulness will lead to divine fruitfulness—a fruitfulness defined by righteousness, compassion and peace rather than by numbers, appearances and attractiveness."

Bryan Chapell, Pastor
Grace Presbyterian Church, Peoria, IL

"This book is a clarion call for every believer to return from the worldly path of control, idolatry and pride to the kingdom path of humility, love and stewardship in his or her life and ministry. I was especially impressed with its stress upon radical generosity. I highly recommend this book to every Christian eager to follow Jesus faithfully in this age of crisis when mammonism and prosperity gospel are overwhelmingly prevalent and penetrating even into the church and numerous parachurch ministries. This is a must read!"

Sung Wook Chung, DPhil (Oxford University)
Professor of Christian Theology
and Director of Korean Initiatives, Denver Seminary

"I recommend that every ministry and ministry network works through *The Choice* to determine whether they follow the kingdom path. The excellent study guide and practical resources will help facilitate discussion within team meetings but also during global ministry network gatherings. I hope that this book will become a platform for determining success in all areas of ministry and become essential reading in theological institutions around the world."

Sas Conradie, Coordinator
Lausanne / World Evangelical Alliance Global Generosity Network

"With all the Christian formulas of leadership that simply mimic popular models and smatter them with some Bible, you'll find in *The Choice* a refreshingly different take. Here's a book that starts with the Book and draws the reader into what Christ-centered ministry and leadership should look like."

Barry H. Corey, President
Biola University

"Gary Hoag, Scott Rodin, and Wes Willmer have written an essential resource – a stewardship kit – for every pastor and ministry leader who is tired of 'doing it themselves to death.' *The Choice* is a clear, concise, practical and applicable manual that demonstrates how to create development strategies that focus on faithfulness and results focused on eternity."

Melinda Delahoyde, VP of Strategic Advancement and
Partnerships
Life International

"*The Choice* is a clarion call to forsake the common, natural tendency to do ministry in our own strength, power and initiative and to embrace Christ's heart of ministry to others. John Wesley, states 'a fanatic is one who seeks desired ends while ignoring the constituted means to reach those ends.'… I am convicted at how easily I ignore 'Christ's constituted means' for growing His church. Thanks for the timely word and for calling me to what really matters."

Randy Discher, Senior Pastor,
Constance Free Church, Andover, MN

"The authors of *The Choice* challenge ministry leaders and board members to rethink approaches, motivations, planning processes, and assessment outcomes in light of kingdom understandings of leadership and stewardship. In this well-conceived, reader-friendly, insightful, and highly applicable work, Hoag, Rodin, and Willmer chart the course for churches and parachurch ministries, as well as institutions and organizations, to once again refocus all activities and strategies in accordance with biblical faithfulness. I was certainly helped by this book and I trust numerous others will be as well."

David S. Dockery, President
Trinity International University

"When it comes to running our churches and ministries, it requires a consuming adoration for the Savior not to become seduced by the ways of our culture. *The Choice* helps us turn away from those siren calls that can drown out the Spirit's guiding whispers, "This is what Jesus meant; here is the kingdom path; just walk in it. This book is so timely for today's Christian leaders – I highly recommend it!"

Joni Eareckson Tada, Founder
Joni and Friends International Disability Center

"A remarkable book that will unleash those pursuing a Christ-centered life for maximum kingdom impact. By exploring and following practical formational practices of Christ's ministry revealed by the authors, a life of fruitfulness will be your legacy."

Steve Fedyski, President & CEO
Pinnacle Forum

"Over the years in Christian camping ministry, I have often felt the pressure to perform and achieve success based on a secular, production-driven model. Gary, Scott, and Wes bring another option – a renewed and profound thinking guided by Scripture and God's leading. *The Choice* is a must-read by everyone in leadership; best done as you sit before God, listen for His guidance, and humbly submit to His direction."

Peter Fiorello, Executive Director
Camp Spofford

"*The Choice* will challenge hearts of all who are ministry-focused for the glory of God and desire to follow Christ-centered principles from the pages of Scripture. In doing so, churches and Christian organizations can work as unto the Lord for the purpose of pointing people to Jesus Christ as Lord and Savior—that is *the choice* that really counts for eternity."

Franklin Graham, President & CEO, Samaritan's Purse
and Billy Graham Evangelistic Association

"We have often felt suffocated by the outcomes, metrics, and results demanded from us as leaders. Many times we have wondered, 'Is this what it means to lead a Christian ministry?' While reading *The Choice*, we felt like the two men walking to Emmaus with Jesus explaining everything to us through the Scriptures. After reading it we said, 'were not our hearts burning within us while on the road (of leadership)?' We knew it! There is a Christian way and you too can find it in *The Choice*! We urge you to translate this book to other languages."

Edgar and Gladys Güitz, Executive Directors,
Potter's House Association International
27 years serving among the scavenger community in Guatemala
City garbage dump

"*The Choice* is the rare book that combines prophetic witness and practical ministry application with clarity and spiritual depth. Hoag, Rodin, and Willmer have crafted a manifesto for Christ-centered ministry. This book is an ideal resource for leaders and boards grappling with faithful service in a production-oriented culture."

Jeff Haanen, Executive Director
Denver Institute for Faith & Work

"Hoag, Rodin, and Willmer make a vital case for achieving mission in a way that honors how God designed us as leaders. Results in ministry, while seemingly fundamental to our calling, are sacred evidence of God's work rather than a badge of honor and credibility for ourselves. *The Choice* provides us with a clear and tactical path to surrender control over our ministries and pursue a leadership character which redefines sustainability as 'maintaining a posture of dependence on the Father.' I'm privileged to recommend this book and accompanying study guide with high esteem."

Daryl Heald, Founder
Global Generosity Movement

"Hoag, Rodin, and Willmer are to be commended for their work in this book. It calls us to recognize the ways in which we have put our mission before God's mission and therefore created leadership models focused on personal rather than kingdom outcomes. All who read this book will be challenged to examine the way they lead, edified by the practical and formational processes outlined herein, and encouraged by the reality that God reigns!"

Greg Henson, President
Sioux Falls Seminary

"Whether leading churches or planting new churches, *The Choice* is an essential tool to give you focus doing kingdom work in kingdom ways. I can't wait to communicate the time-honored, kingdom-oriented, joy-filled, Holy Spirit guided way of doing life together with those in the Anglican Mission and my local church. This book carefully articulates kingdom values God has sewn in my heart and life. Read, learn, mark and inwardly digest everything in this book."

Rt. Rev. Philip H. Jones, Senior Pastor, All Saints Church Dallas,
Missionary Bishop and Apostolic Vicar-Elect, Anglican Mission

"Worldliness can take all sorts of forms, even in Christian ministry, and in this book Hoag, Rodin, and Willmer challenge us to make a choice to turn from the assumptions that the world presses upon us and to embrace a better way—the way of Jesus and His Kingdom. Anyone involved in Christian leadership will profit from this reminder that you can gain the whole world but forfeit you soul."

Bill Kynes, Pastor
Cornerstone Evangelical Free Church, Annandale, VA

"Jesus was, and still is, the ultimate leader! Jesus exemplified the leader as a Shepherd, a Servant and a Steward. Hoag, Rodin, and Willmer give us a wonderful picture of a steward leader. Each gentleman has spent a lifetime of making application of the contents in this book. This is not theory to them but the sharing of a lifetime of experiences. Gary, Scott, and Wes, thank you so much for this contribution to any leader's tool box!

Lauren Libby, International President & CEO
TWR International

"*The Choice* belongs on the reading list of every Christian leader. It may be the most liberating leadership book I've ever read. It frees us from the chains of earthly measurement and challenges us to examine how God measures the success of our endeavors – and how we should, too. Perhaps best of all, I have the privilege of knowing the authors personally, and I can testify that these are no armchair theologians. They have tested these lessons in their lives and work."

Jim Liske, President & CEO
Prison Fellowship Ministries

"Scripture provides guidelines and principles by which we can experience a break out of God's Kingdom in our individual, church and ministry lives. *The Choice* does an excellent job of identifying what Christ-centered success and leadership looks like and offers some practical steps on how to make changes in our personal and professional lives, to better align with Scripture."

Gerard Long, Executive Director
Alpha USA

"*The Choice* is a watershed book on leadership. Not the run-of-the-mill leadership but one that clearly defines, as well as models, leading from a kingdom perspective. This is radical leadership desperately needed for the second decade of 21st century."

Jo Anne Lyon, General Superintendent
The Wesleyan Church

"All three of these authors with Ph.D.'s are known nationally and even internationally as thought leaders in the areas of leadership, governance, New Testament, theology, and generosity as they speak, write and publish individually. Anytime the three combine their efforts and expertise, I recommend paying attention to the practical wisdom that results."

Elisa Morgan, Speaker
Author, *The Beauty of Broken*

"Yikes! Stop the presses! Stop the rat race! Push pause! Lead your team and your board, chapter by chapter, through this powerful poke in the spiritual ribs—until you can align your B.H.A.G., your strategic plan, and your results with God's path (not yours)."

John Pearson, Author,
*Mastering the Management Buckets*

"Reading a book by Gary Hoag and Scott Rodin is to know that some of my paradigms will be challenged. In their book, *The Sower*, my view of fundraising activities were challenged and reordered. Now joined by Wesley Willmer they are at it again in *The Choice*, causing me to reexamine our goals and measurement of success and daring me to take a path toward kingdom outcomes, not those prescribed by the world."

Bob Snyder MD, President,
International Health Services

"I just about used an entire highlighter. The book starts strong, with excellent observations that distinguish between the world's view of success and what the Bible and the life of Christ have to say. Then, it gets stronger with so many profound questions and practical ways to move toward the viewpoint of Scripture. Honestly, this book describes the way I know I should lead and the way that I want to lead, but too often don't lead. However, I didn't feel like the book was beating me up, I felt like it was lifting me up and encouraging me to press on, seek true success and lead well. I so concur with the book's viewpoint that unexamined presuppositions drive everything we, as leaders, do. The myriad of voices in our culture drive us to almost instinctively measure success by 'more' instead of by flourishing biblically. The ten marks of Christ-centered ministry are clear, practical and convicting. This isn't a book that I will just read; it is a book that I can use to help me be a more Christ-centered leader."

David Wills, President
National Christian Foundation

# THE
# CHOICE

*The Christ-Centered Pursuit
of Kingdom Outcomes*

Gary G. Hoag, R. Scott Rodin, & Wesley K. Willmer

ECFA.org/ECFAPress.aspx

Cover: *Starry Night*, Vincent Van Gogh

Scripture quotations are from the New International Version of the Bible.

ISBN: 978-1-936233-20-5

# Foreword

At ECFA, we are passionate about helping churches and ministries accomplish God's work in a manner that bears much fruit and brings God glory! To accomplish these overarching objectives, we set high standards of integrity to which churches and other Christ-centered nonprofit organizations voluntarily agree to follow.

It is a privilege for ECFAPress to publish this book which addresses what may be the most important and yet most unexamined presupposition related to ministry today – defining success. Improper views of success can fundamentally impact how organizations address the three pillars on which ECFA focuses: governance, financial management, and fundraising/stewardship decisions. Boards can lapse into strategic decisions without discerning God's will, financial statements can be crafted simply to attain a high ranking with rating organizations, and resource-raising can stoop to employing marginally deceptive practices.

Secular values beckon us to adopt the world's way of thinking linked to most everything we do, and often we conform to cultural norms without even knowing it. There is the continual push for higher and greater results. To achieve them our ministry leadership teams need a seemingly endless supply of money to try to make ministry happen.

To explore these issues, we asked three trusted friends who know God's Word and understand its application in our world to assist us. Their task: determine how we got where we are and map a Christ-centered course for people to take that is biblically faithful and that positions the ministries we serve for fruitfulness.

They exceeded our expectations. We expected a resource from them. Based on what came from their study, we believe this work could contribute to a revival. We pray it will catalyze a Great Awakening worldwide among leaders and lay people in churches and everyone from executives to employees in ministries.

Why are we so enthusiastic about this resource? This book identifies the current situation, suggests how we got here, and contains literally dozens of practical, formational insights for life and leadership. The principles embedded in this book provide a Christ-centered path for pursuing kingdom outcomes. It also contains a study guide for going through the material in small group settings as well as tools for working through the concepts with boards and leadership teams. It is easy to read and, more importantly, it is relevant to all Christ-followers engaged in God's work. We could not be more pleased to be publishing this book.

In a timely fashion, *The Choice* offers a timeless, biblical response to prevailing practices and helps us experience the transformation that comes from renewing our minds and committing our lives to a Christ-centered path.

Don't just read this book. Make the choice to follow the kingdom path!

*Therefore, I urge you, brothers and sisters, in view of God's mercy, to offer your bodies as a living sacrifice, holy and pleasing to God—this is your true and proper worship. Do not conform to the pattern of this world, but be transformed by the renewing of your mind. Then you will be able to test and approve what God's will is—His good, pleasing and perfect will.* Romans 12:1-2

Dan Busby
President
ECFA

# Preface

If I could commend one book to anyone involved in church or ministry work today, whether serving in a paid position or volunteer capacity, it would be this book. This includes everyone in the Christian Leadership Alliance!

As I interact with pastors and leaders whose churches or ministries are flourishing, their paradigm or approach to ministry is strikingly similar to the kingdom path outlined in this book.

For many others, I believe they would admit that somewhere in the course of leadership, either the world's way of thinking got them rolling down the common path or they succumbed to one or more of the three temptations that Christ faced before launching His earthly ministry.

For example, some share that they are exhausted and stressed from trying to deliver metrics that they cannot control. Others testify to feeling like all they do is chase money to stay open. Many have become disillusioned with the state of ministry today and, as a result, they want out. This list of challenges goes on and on.

What I love about this book is that it not only assesses our current situation, it shows how we may have gotten to this place and suggests the choice all leaders must make to get on track.

I especially appreciate the way in which Gary, Scott, and Wes are able to humbly identify the characteristics of the common path and the temptations we face because they themselves have battled those temptations. From their biblical knowledge and leadership experiences, they make the complicated simple. Without dodging the difficulties leaders face, they chart a Christ-centered course for pursuing kingdom outcomes.

This book is light in darkness. It puts things in perspective and helps us see clearly.

The way it maps for us isn't just a road to freedom. It is a path to maturity, which sometimes results in fruitfulness and other times, suffering, but always results in faithfulness, which the authors make abundantly clear from Scripture, is all God asks of us.

I believe the kingdom path is the only course we can take if we desire to see kingdom outcomes in our churches and ministry settings. I have adopted the rule of life and roadmap for pursuing kingdom outcomes outlined in the resources section at the end of the book and hope you do too.

Not only do I consider the authors as wise advisors, they are my friends. They wrote this book to help you and me. It is readable, biblical and practical. Share it with anyone you know in ministry. And more importantly, make the choice! Do what it says.

*Be very careful, then, how you live — not as unwise but as wise, making the most of every opportunity, because the days are evil.*
Ephesians 5:15-16

Tami Heim
CEO
Christian Leadership Alliance

# Table of Contents

# Introduction

These are challenging times for churches and ministries. Prominent voices like Richard Stearns (*Unfinished*), David Platt (*Radical*), Shane Claiborne (*The Irresistible Revolution*), and Kyle Idleman (*Not a Fan*) have noted that American churches and ministry leaders may be headed in the wrong direction. Reports reveal that the global church also wants answers. Are we lost?

Recently, David Platt released a sequel to *Radical* entitled *Radical Together*. The aim of that book is stated in a single question: "How can we in the church best unleash the people of God in the Spirit of God with the Word of God for the glory of God in the world?"[1] We believe the answer lies in God's people discovering their way from Scripture and choosing the right path.

This book is about recalculating the route for Christ-centered ministry. Its underlying assumption is that far too many churches and ministries operate according to unexamined presuppositions that drive everything they do. When we examined them, we found that the way we define and measure success has much to do with how we got to the precarious place we find ourselves. Our definitions of success shape what we say, think, and do.

Chapter one introduces the two paths we believe most people take based on how they define and measure success. The common path reflects what most everyone is doing. People on this path are driven to do whatever is required to deliver results measured by church growth and ministry expansion using all the resources they can muster. Alternatively, the kingdom path outlines what we believe God expects of each of us. There are those who think as Christ-followers we can do both—that is, rely on our own strength to make things happen for God and live lives of humble obedience to God. What we have discovered is that if we go after the former, we miss the mark because we are aiming at the wrong target. When we idolize results that we think please Him, we actually fail to exhibit the obedience He asks of us. If instead we pursue the kingdom path, then fruitfulness, or kingdom outcomes, are the by-product. The kingdom path is the *only* path that leads to kingdom outcomes.

Chapter two offers three ways we end up on the common path. The evil one tempts us to take control, to trust in what we can see, and to revel in the praise people give us when we excel. These values not only drive our world but they may also be hindering our fruitfulness for the kingdom. The three deceptions that face ministry leaders and Christ-followers are the same three temptations that preceded the ministry of Jesus. What we endeavor to do in chapters three, four, and five is learn from Jesus to discern how we should respond. In so doing, we conclude that the reason the Spirit led Jesus to be tempted was to show us how to overcome the devil's deceptions. As these three victories paved the way for the ministry of Jesus, they must precede ours.

So what should ministry look like? Jesus instructs us to follow Him. When we do, we find ten marks, or characteristics, from Christ's earthly ministry that are also evident in the early church. Chapter six contains these ten marks and includes practical formational practices to help us follow the kingdom path. If this sounds oversimplified to you, candidly, we think we are the ones who have complicated things. Remember, Jesus recruited ordinary, mostly uneducated people and gave them basic instructions. He used words like "follow," "trust," and "obey." Are we simply meeting those clear requests?

We realize this book may call each of us to make changes both personally and professionally, so chapter seven includes a study guide and resources for pursuing kingdom outcomes. We have included these practical tools to help Christ-followers understand and apply the principles in this book individually, in small groups, as well as in larger ministry settings. We pray you journey through this book with an open mind, willing to go where the Spirit leads.

You will notice that we chose Van Gogh's famous *Starry Night* for our cover image. The significance of this image cannot be understated. Gaze into it. While the heavens proclaim God's glory and a few homes flicker with light, the church positioned in the center is dark. Sadly, this depicts the reality in many places today. Many churches and ministries need the power restored and the lights turned on. Our prayer is that this book helps do just that in the dark times we find ourselves. That will only happen if, together, we make the choice to take the kingdom path.

*But if serving the LORD seems undesirable to you, then choose for yourselves this day whom you will serve, whether the gods your forefathers served beyond the River, or the gods of the Amorites, in whose land you are living. But as for me and my household, we will serve the LORD.* Joshua 24:15

Gary G. Hoag, Ph.D.
R. Scott Rodin, Ph.D.
Wesley K. Willmer, Ph.D.

## Chapter One

# How Do We Define and Measure Success?

*"The value of our life does not depend*
*on the place we occupy.*
*It depends on the way we occupy that place."[2]*
Thérèse de Lisieux

Defining success may be the most important decision we make as God's people. Measuring it comes a close second because what we measure communicates what we value. How leaders define and measure success gives form and direction to all aspects of ministry. It shapes the culture that follows and ultimately determines our future.

In the world of ministry today, we believe people define and measure success in one of two ways. While there may be variations to these scenarios, the guiding force for every congregation or organization appears to reflect one of two paths. As both demand full allegiance, we demonstrate that these two options are mutually exclusive. Each demands total allegiance. The choice regarding which path to take is ours to make.

## OPTION #1: THE COMMON PATH

We use the term "common" to label this path because it is the one most churches and ministries are taking. On this path, pastors and ministry leaders define success in terms of results, which are commonly linked to levels of church growth or ministry expansion. This definition drives leaders to focus on the never-ending expansion of their work. Boards reinforce this assumption by holding leaders accountable for the growth metrics that measure this expansion. Results are typically measured in three ways: (1) Some report numerical increases in clients or customers: more students, more missionaries in the field, more church members, and more people served by our services. (2) Others evaluate growth in the form of physical expansion: more or larger facilities, new venues, and launching an online presence, etc. (3) Many measure success in financial terms: larger budgets, greater gift income, growing endowments, and broadening sources of support.

When God's people make the choice to define success in terms of these outputs, such as church growth or ministry expansion, it sends the church or ministry down a predictable path. That path can be described according to the following five characteristics that fall like dominoes from this definition. This chart illustrates the common path. The description for each characteristic follows.

| The Common Path |
|---|
| Production-Driven Leadership |
| Expansion-Focused Strategies |
| Earthly Oriented Metrics |
| Results-Based Management |
| Utilitarian View of Resources |

## Production-Driven Leadership

Leaders are recruited, employed, valued, and rewarded by their ability to lead an organization through a continual process of expansion. They are valued for pursuing quantitative metrics and delivering yearly increases. To do so they lead in a production-oriented fashion. They tend to emphasize tangible expressions of growth on personal, community, and organization levels.

Production-driven leaders often surround themselves with people who are similarly wired. This contributes to the formation of a hard-driving culture that places the highest value on ends (the results produced) and a lesser value on means (how those results are produced).

## Expansion-Focused Strategies

Production-driven leaders devise expansion-focused strategies. These strategies deploy human and financial resources to accomplish the desired levels of growth. While there are undoubtedly some qualitative components to the overall organizational strategy, those components must yield to the work of achieving desired ends within the confines of the staff and budget. Thus, strategies that focus on the quality of work are, in the end, made subservient to the larger vision of expansion.

The underlying assumption is that in order to do our work better, we must do more of it. Growth is the unexamined presupposition, the driving force in our definition of success. As a result, strategic plans are written to articulate what "more" looks like in quantifiable terms. On this path, leaders tend to overwork high-functioning staff and minimize the role others play because they think they don't have what it takes to make things happen. While quality may be important, it often must give way to the increased pressure to post ever-growing results.

### Earthly Oriented Metrics

Organizations that measure success in these terms develop measurements and metrics associated with their expansion-focused strategies. These metrics are temporal in nature and counted in three primary areas: people, facilities, and finances. The influence of these metrics goes beyond these three areas and finds its way into human resource procedures, core values statements, and board governance policies. As such, every area of organizational life becomes aligned with quantifiable church growth or ministry expansion.

Performance at every level—from the individual to the team and the leadership to the board—is assessed according to one overarching goal: numbers. Church and ministry professionals today can acquire a host of applications and management tools that measure different factors that contribute to growth. They promise to increase production and achieve desired results, and so they are highly valued by those on this path.

### Results-Based Management

When leaders define success in terms of church growth or ministry expansion, the organizational management systems adjust to align with that definition. Management training, pay scales, incentives, discipline, and promotion depend on each employee's ability to help the organization reach its goals, execute its strategies, and deliver metrics. From the perspective of prevailing governance models, this is referred to as "controlling ends."

The perceived ability of a person to control ends becomes the highest value in managerial assessment and promotion as well as board recruitment. Any initiative that cannot be directly aligned with these stated ends is automatically devalued. Peripheral activities may persist in faith-based organizations, but these activities, and often the people who perform them, will likely be regarded as secondary and auxiliary to the primary work and positions that fuel growth.

## Utilitarian View of Resources

Production-driven leaders often regard the human and financial resources available to them as assets. Though they describe their work as stewardship, they minimize the intrinsic value of the resources entrusted to them. While this sounds harsh, it follows that the value of assets is directly linked with their ability to help the ministry achieve its bottom line.

Because growth requires a never-ending stream of raw material, the drive to secure increased supply seems insatiable. Any means of securing them may be tolerated and even justified (*It's for the kingdom!*), in the same way that employee policies, management, strategies, metrics, and characteristics of leadership may have all been compromised in the process of producing greater levels of growth.

## Summary: The Common Path

When we define success along the lines of the common path, that choice charts a familiar course that shapes the future. The activities of most of our ministries reflect that we are on this path, whether we outwardly say so or not. We employ production-oriented leaders who implement expansion-focused strategies evaluated with output-oriented metrics. Moreover, we function by way of results-based management and demonstrate a utilitarian view of resources. We do all this to deliver results in the form of church growth and ministry expansion.

If we were secular leaders running a business, we might deem this acceptable. Since we are participating in the work of the Lord, might we come to a different conclusion? Phil Vischer, founder and former CEO of VeggieTales, thinks so:

> We're drinking a cocktail that's a mix of the Protestant work ethic, the American dream, and the gospel. And we've intertwined them so completely that we can't tell them apart anymore. Our gospel has become a gospel of following your dreams and being good so God will make all your dreams come true…So I had to peel that apart. I realized I'm not supposed to be pursuing impact. I'm supposed to be pursuing God. And when I pursue God I will have exactly as much impact as He wants me to have.[3]

Have we, too, been pursuing the wrong thing? Have we mistakenly idolized the results that we thought pleased God and in so doing failed to please Him altogether? Since we are producing results for God, they are kingdom outcomes, right? Or are they?

We believe it's time to ask larger questions. Is the drive to control ends biblical? If it is not, then where did it come from? In taking the common path, have we adopted a worldly, possibly even antibiblical understanding of life and leadership when viewed in light of God's order of things? Did we, without realizing it, abandon the values of the kingdom by taking the common path and defining success in terms of growth and expansion? Do we have another option? Is there another path we can take?

## OPTION #2: THE KINGDOM PATH

On this path, success is defined in terms of our obedience to the instructions of Jesus Christ for which He promises eternal rewards. On the kingdom path, we as Christ-followers become less concerned about results that we cannot control because our primary concern is obedience. Our attention shifts from what we are doing for God to what God asks us to do and wants to accomplish in and through us. The former represents results we think we can generate taking the common path; the latter reflects the kingdom outcomes God produces through faithful followers.

How would we measure success along these lines? The kingdom path still assesses three ministry measures—people, facilities, and finances—but it does so in radically different ways. Each of these relate to individuals as well as congregations and organizations: (1) Quantitative measurements that count clients or people served are superseded with qualitative measurements of our own faithfulness in meeting needs (*How many?* vs. *How well?*). (2) The focus on expansion of facilities shifts to considering our effectiveness in stewarding the resources we have (*How do we build more?* vs. *What are we doing with what we have?*). (3) The drive for financial growth and security that leads to hoarding under the guise of sustainability is supplanted by the desire to maintain a posture of dependence on God (*How can we secure our present and our future?* vs. *Are we trusting God to provide for our current needs and for the future by putting to work what He provides?*).

What would it look like to go this direction today? The Christ-follower who takes the kingdom path walks headlong into the blowing gale of the common path mindset that dominates church and ministry cultures. Let's look at the same five traits that flow from defining success in terms of obedience to the teachings of Jesus. This chart outlines them; their descriptions follow.

| The Kingdom Path |
| :---: |
| Steward Leadership |
| Faithfulness-Focused Strategies |
| Eternity-Oriented Metrics |
| Relationship-Based Management |
| Stewardship View of Resources |

**Steward Leadership**

Steward leaders are not driven by production. They are Christ-followers who depend on God to produce everything. They are recruited according to their Christ-like character and evaluated according to their ability to lead an organization in ways that reflect Christ-centered values, strategies, plans, and actions (cf. 1 Corinthians 4:1–2).

Steward leaders have set aside the need for increased reputation, personal financial rewards and organizational renown and are motivated by promise of eternal rewards linked to faithfulness. While production-driven leaders focus on ends and are celebrated for delivering results, steward leaders focus on the goal of unwavering obedience to the Master's instructions and give Him the glory for whatever fruit He produces.

This does not mean that production-driven leaders are not obedient, or that steward leaders will not report the results of measured growth and increased impact. The key difference is the force that guides them. Steward leaders cannot be driven by church growth or ministry expansion and obedience simultaneously. One path will always take priority over the other! They must choose one or the other.

## Faithfulness-Focused Strategies

Steward leaders who are singularly motivated by obedience adopt faithfulness-focused strategies. Like Jesus, they desire to say what the Father says to say and do what the Father says to do (cf. John 5:19; 14:10). Discerning and doing God's will are their primary strategies. They serve with humble transparency for the sake of accountability. They understand the instructions of Jesus, model obedience to the same, and exhort others to follow them as they follow Christ.

Steward leaders also believe the good works they and others perform at the church or ministry are worthless before God unless the Holy Spirit generates them. They are determined to embrace faithfulness-focused strategies because they realize obedience over time is the only path for producing kingdom outcomes. In biblical terms, they realize that no branch can bear fruit unless it remains attached to the vine (cf. John 15:4). They realize that fruit is not the result of our strategic labors but rather the kingdom outcomes that flow from our obedience.

## Eternity-Oriented Metrics

Steward leaders use eternity-oriented metrics to measure the effectiveness of faithfulness-focused strategies. They tend to be more qualitative than quantitative. For example, Jesus called twelve disciples and instructed them to make disciples. He defined that not with quantifiable evangelistic goals (such as number of souls saved), but with the qualitative imperative that they teach people to observe or obey everything Jesus had taught them (cf. Matthew 28:19–20). Another key difference is that eternity-oriented metrics measure growth in God's kingdom, not in any earthly one.

The key to grasping eternity-oriented metrics is realizing that the quantitative is subordinate to the qualitative. Could this be why the modern church has so many professing Christians and so few disciples of Jesus Christ? Have we been focusing on counting decisions instead of making disciples? Leaders who employ eternity-oriented metrics will transform the ministry culture and shape everything from human resource policies to decisions regarding asset use, partnerships and collaborations, board governance, and financial practices.

### Relationship-Based Management

Management practices on this path focus on the quality of relationships rather than the quantity of outputs. In plain terms, the desire of Jesus is that we are known by our love, not our numbers (cf. John 13:35)! This does not mean that clear measurements of performance are jettisoned—in fact quite the opposite is true. Relationship-based management looks at people as children of God and not as components in a process of producing a tangible end result in pursuit of a strategy of growth and expansion.

Steward leaders show respect to people as fellow pilgrims on life's journey by humbly serving them rather than lording over them. In so doing, they exhibit Christ-centered values in community. Rather than loving money and using people to produce results, they demonstrate a love for people and the obedient use of money in accordance with the Master's instructions. Their identity is rooted in Jesus Christ, not position or prominence. They trust that God will guide and bless the ministry as He sees fit, and all the while they pursue obedience.

### Stewardship View of Resources

Steward leaders relate to the human and financial resources in their management as stewards rather than as owners. They help people discern their spiritual gifts and deploy themselves in kingdom service (cf. 2 Timothy 1:6). Staff members are hired according to their giftedness, and promoted and rewarded for faithfulness.

The stewardship of financial resources is linked to putting what we have to work. Steward leaders do not view assets as a source of security or a means of production. Instead, they seek God's guidance for the most faithful and appropriate way to deploy His resources. They exhibit generosity and a biblical disdain for hoarding with a vigilance never to let the security or hope of the ministry shift from God to the quantity of their resources. To put it simply, leaders on this path will not allow the church or ministry they serve to shift from serving God to serving money.

### Summary: The Kingdom Path

When Christ-followers choose the path of obedience, their primary motivation becomes attaining eternal rewards rather than achieving earthly results. This shift in priorities influences everything else in life and leadership. On this path, steward leaders are hired for their Christ-like character and assessed for keeping the church or ministry aligned with God's purposes. They strategically target faithfulness and evaluate efforts with qualitative, eternity-oriented metrics. Such leaders value people and steward resources in a manner that reflects obedience to the teachings of Jesus regardless of the results.

We believe the kingdom path reflects the biblical instructions for all Christ-followers. It requires faith to implement. While this approach may be generally accepted in principle, it is not widely practiced.

### Exploring the Kingdom Path and Making the Choice

We invite you to join us in exploring the kingdom path. John Calvin suggested that such activity helps us stay on track: "He who has learned to look to God in everything he does is at the same time diverted from all vain thoughts."[4] The best way we can avoid the potholes, unnecessary detours, and rabbit trails of ministry is to consider thoughtfully the instructions set forth for us in Scripture. This includes testing the prevailing practices of the world by God's Word. However, our exploration must not stop there. This knowledge must drive us to make hard decisions, regardless of what others are doing. The common path is named just that because so many are on it. Following Christ requires us to go against the crowd. Making choices is important in the Christian faith. Few articulate the significance more powerfully than Chuck Colson:

> Tonight you have to make your choice. Every man, every woman, every boy and every girl, you will have to make your choice between pleasure and Christ, amusements and Christ, popularity and Christ, money and Christ. Whatever is keeping you from the kingdom of God, you will have to make a choice tonight, and if you refuse to make the choice, that very act means you have already made it.[5]

Some have made the choice to follow the kingdom path. Far too many others have chosen the common path that conforms to the patterns and practices of this world. Starting today, we invite you to join us on a journey that will take you down the kingdom path. Why make this choice today? Because we believe the kingdom path represents the only route from which we can faithfully pursue kingdom outcomes.

No matter what others say or do, we are calling God's people—from pastors to parishioners and executives to employees—to define success in terms of obedience to the teachings of Jesus. And as we have seen, this choice not only shapes all of life and leadership but it influences every aspect of ministry and the fruitfulness that follows.

When we embrace the kingdom path, everything changes: the questions change, the metrics change, the focus changes, the strategies change, the culture changes. The full attention shifts to God's bigger picture, because obedience is the bigger picture. Can we make a case for why we would have any other definition?

The chart below summarizes the ground we have covered thus far. Which path are you on? Which list best describes your church or ministry? We pray you will make an honest appraisal of your attitudes and practices and seek God's guidance for the way ahead.

| The Common Path | The Kingdom Path |
|---|---|
| Production-Driven Leadership | Steward Leadership |
| Expansion-Focused Strategies | Faithfulness-Focused Strategies |
| Earthly Oriented Metrics | Eternity-Oriented Metrics |
| Results-Based Management | Relationship-Based Management |
| Utilitarian View of Resources | Stewardship View of Resources |

In the next chapter we will sketch what we believe are the roots of this desire for delivering growing results. We will also suggest ways that we as Christ-followers can obediently stay on the kingdom path.

# Chapter Two

# The Lies of the Enemy: Three Temptations We All Face

*If you read history you will find that the Christians who did most for the present world were just those who thought most of the next...*
*It is since Christians have largely ceased to think of the other world that they have become so ineffective in this.*
*Aim at Heaven and you will get earth "thrown in":*
*aim at earth and you will get neither.*[6] C. S. Lewis

What are we aiming at?

From the first moments of creation, the enemy has been lying to us. He lied to the first couple, promising them equality with God. He tricked the kings and rulers of Israel and Judah in the Old Testament to think that compromise and comingling with false religions would lead to peace and prosperity. He deceived priests and prophets, military commanders, and commoners into thinking that the performance of empty rituals was what pleased God.

Scripture calls him "the father of lies" and when we fall into his traps, we limit our effectiveness here on earth. When he succeeds in getting us to aim at the wrong target, we always miss the mark!

At the risk of oversimplifying, we believe we can summarize the substance of this history of deception into three categories: control, idolatry, and pride. They are listed with synonymous terms in 1 John 2:15–17 as "the lust of the flesh, the lust of the eyes, and the pride of life."

> *Do not love the world or anything in the world. If anyone loves the world, love for the Father is not in them. For everything in the world—the lust of the flesh, the lust of the eyes, and the pride of life—comes not from the Father but from the world. The world and its desires pass away, but whoever does the will of God lives forever.*

Interestingly, John set these three sins—control, idolatry, and pride—in contrast to those who obey or do God's will, and likewise, these three sins mirror the temptations over which Jesus was victorious prior to His earthly ministry. They also appear as the gateway to the common path.

Has the enemy been effective in leading us to embrace the common path and, in doing so, actually diverted our energy and limited our fruitfulness for God's kingdom? Let's look more closely at each one and the impact it has on God's work.

## Deception #1: Control ("the Lust of the Flesh")

The first deception plays on our natural desire for self-determination. We like to be in control, manage our affairs and determine our own destiny. This is nothing new, as we see people fall to this temptation throughout the Scriptures.

Adam and Eve were promised the power of the knowledge of good and evil, power to decide for themselves what was good and take control from the hands of their Creator. In response to a God who had given them everything they could ever want, they grasped at the chance to judge for themselves. In doing so they found that God had, indeed, chosen what was good. They also found that they were now vulnerable to the evil that God had rejected for them in His sovereignty. They gained control but lost intimacy with God.

For a leadership example, consider the role of Moses in getting water to God's thirsty people in the wilderness. In Exodus 17, God instructed him to strike the rock. The Hebrew word for "rock" in that geographic context points to granite, through which no water could flow by means of striking; thus, striking the rock and having water flow was an act of obedience that brought glory to God. Moses did it and the outcome was truly a miracle.

In Numbers 20:1–13, the setting was different. God told Moses to speak to the rock. Our English translations again render it simply, "rock," but this Hebrew word used this time is associated with limestone. Why does this matter? If someone wanted to find water in that part of the desert, they would hit the porous limestone a few times. Unlike with the granite, striking would work here. That's just what Moses did! Instead of speaking to it, he hit the rock twice. His disobedience shows he took matters into his own hands. God told him to speak to the rock so that when water flowed God would again receive glory. For ignoring God's instructions and taking control of the situation, Moses was disqualified from leadership. Elsewhere we find other examples in Scripture where God's people succumb to the whispers of the enemy and try to make things happen with their own strength, rather than following God's instructions (cf. Abram and Sarai in Genesis 16).

With this first deception comes the first conflict between the world's values and the values of God's kingdom. The former relies on self-determination and places our destiny on our shoulders; whereas the latter calls us to a posture of dependence on God, surrendering control and following Him in obedience as He determines our future. This is a fundamental conflict. God's people do not have the option of both/and. This holds true both in life and leadership.

We cannot follow Jesus in our personal lives while in professional ministry settings we function as though we think our role is to wield power, to make things happen, and to rely on our own strength and ability. Alternatively, what would it look like to relinquish control? For starters, it requires us to reject this first lie of the enemy. In chapter three, we explore this temptation further.

## Deception #2: Idolatry ("the Lust of the Eyes")

The second deception is idolatry. We are guilty of this sin when we trust in what we can see rather than in God, whom we cannot see. Our idols are whatever we depend on in place of God. As one leader put it, our idol is whatever we use as a safety net in times of crisis. Do we have any safety net other than God? For most of us, it is money or possessions.

Money is the one thing most of the world seeks after because the world says money solves all problems (cf. Ecclesiastes 10:19). No wonder greed and covetousness are so pervasive. Conversely, in God's economy, the reason Christ-followers are neither to store up treasures on earth nor worry about what we will eat, drink, or wear is because the Father in heaven knows we need these things and has promised to supply them for those who seek Him first. When God's people obediently put our trust in Him instead of money and He supplies our ongoing needs and the resources for our generosity, He gets all glory!

Should we ever find ourselves in need, we are not to look to money, possessions, or people with money and possessions to solve our problems, but to the Father. To direct hope anywhere else is idolatrous thinking! If this sounds challenging, it was equally difficult for the first disciples to grasp.

Consider the account of the feeding of the five thousand found in all four Gospels (cf. Matthew 14:13–21; Mark 6:30–44; Luke 9:10–17; John 6:1–14). The disciples thought the needs of the hungry people could only be met if they had two hundred days' wages. Their response shows that they thought money was the solution to their crisis. How did Jesus respond? He took what they had—five loaves and two fish offered by a young boy—and He prayed. The Father multiplied it and provided more than enough for the people to eat.

What is the lesson for Christ-followers? If you need something, ask the Father. Don't look to money to solve your problems. You cannot serve God and money. You cannot have both an abundance mindset and a scarcity mentality simultaneously. God is a God of abundance and the world's way of thinking is linked to scarcity. When we trust in what we can see, we always have a scarcity view. When we place our trust in God, we find His abundance is incomprehensible.

Here's where things get tricky. When we, as Christ-followers, use money that God supplies in accordance with instructions in God's Word, it appears to have power. At that point we can inadvertently fall into the trap of thinking we need more of it to sustain ministry. This leads to the sin of the love of money, the root of all kinds of evil (cf. 1 Timothy 6:10). God's leaders must not exhibit this vice (cf. 1 Timothy 3:3).

When we think of the love of money, our minds often envision greedy Wall Street tycoons, money-grubbing despots or selfish characters like Scrooge in *A Christmas Carol* by Charles Dickens. To enhance your view of this biblical idea, consider this first-century example:

[Those] who are possessed by that grievous malady, [the love of money], though they have no wealth of their own on which they may bestow worship as its due, pay awe-struck homage to that of their neighbors, and come at early dawn to the houses of those who have abundance of it as though they were the grandest temples, there to make their prayers and beg for blessing from the masters as though they were gods. To such He says elsewhere, "Ye shall not follow idols and ye shall not make molten gods," thus teaching them in a figure that it is not fitting to assign divine honors to wealth. (Philo, *Special Laws* I, 24.3)

Most startling is how this description from a contemporary of Jesus looks like the activity of modern-day pastors and ministry leaders who believe that catering to wealthy people is the way to get what they think their congregations or organizations need to make ministry happen. There is certainly a God-honoring, biblical way to invite God's people to participate in God's work through giving, but even then we must never believe that our ministry depends on what they give. To do so is to fall into this trap. Philo calls it what it is: idolatry.

As leaders we must be free from the love of money and resist the temptation to trust in what we can see. This temptation rears its ugly head when we discuss topics like building endowments and maintaining financial sustainability. These may seem like sound financial strategies, but the enemy can twist our attitudes toward them and put us in danger of placing our trust in finances rather than in the Father.

How do we resist this in our lives and leadership? We return to that question again in chapter four, considering how Christ faced and overcame this second temptation.

### Deception #3: Pride ("the Pride of Life")

The third deception plays on our desire for affirmation from people. Put simply, we like being liked. The desire for affirmation is not a negative quality, but when pride dictates our motives, even our best intentions get skewed. Here again we see a mighty clash of values.

We were created to have our identity anchored solely in our relationship to God in Jesus Christ. When we seek our affirmation from God alone, we stand on solid rock in a world of shifting sand. However, when we seek applause from other sources we actually give away our secure place in Christ and exchange it for precarious, momentary fame that we must earn at every turn. This commits us to a life dominated by the pursuit of accolades that feed our desire to be accepted and liked. It's tragic!

In the absence of the assurance of God's love for us, our souls thirst for the reassurance that we are people of worth and that our lives have meaning. In this deception, the enemy keeps us on a performance treadmill in a never-ending pursuit of affirmation. And all the time God is there, extending His unconditional love and offering what we cannot find outside of Him.

Just as individuals can fall prey to this temptation to seek our affirmation from sources apart from Christ, so ministry and church leadership teams can allow jealousy, the desire for worldly praise, the pursuit of reputation, and the thirst for acceptance drive their agendas. What does it look like when a leadership team finds its identity in Christ alone? In chapter five we discern how Jesus resisted this same deception and shows us the course to take when tempted in this way.

## Next Steps

The lure of control, the seduction of idolatry, and the prideful thirst for affirmation make up the enemy's agenda. Jesus offers a different course: to trust in God with our whole heart, to serve Him alone, and to base our identity in relationship to Him. The great cosmic battle is joined over these issues as illustrated below.

| Three Temptations: Control, Idolatry, and Pride | | |
|---|---|---|
| Deception #1 | Deception #2 | Deception #3 |
| "the Lust of the Flesh" | "the Lust of the Eyes" | "the Pride of Life" |
| Who's in control? | Whom do we serve? | In whom will we base our identity? |

Given this comprehensive agenda of the enemy and the countering teachings of Scripture, it should not surprise us that in his face-to-face encounter with the Son of the living God, the enemy attacks on these same three fronts.

In Luke 4:1–13 (cf. Matthew 4:1–11), the Spirit drew Jesus out into the wilderness just prior to the start of His earthly ministry. After Jesus fasted for forty days and nights, the enemy attempted to persuade Jesus with all three lies. In turn, Jesus, bearing our humanity, resisted them and proclaimed victory over the devil. Just as the enemy desired to hinder the ministry of Jesus, he wants to sabotage ours. The same victory Christ won is ours, available to us every day only in the power of the Holy Spirit.

We believe the temptations are recorded for us to understand the enemy's agenda. As God's people, we must follow in the steps of Jesus in our own encounters with the evil one because he has not given up. The enemy uses our sinful culture and its fallen values to create a smokescreen around the truth. This distorts the clarity of kingdom values, causes confusion in our allegiances and clouds the ethics of God's kingdom in the eyes of God's people. Sadly, he has led many astray.

In the next three chapters, we see how Jesus responded to these temptations and examine what they may look like in the context of how we as church and ministry leaders make decisions, set priorities, use resources, develop strategies and, most important, define success.

We believe the greatest challenge facing Christian ministries and churches can be traced to our failure in the face of the three temptations that Jesus overcame for us. By understanding His response to each, we can discover our need for repentance and the power to prevail in the name of Jesus.

Chapter Three

# Stones to Bread:
# The Temptation of Control

*Jesus, full of the Holy Spirit, left the Jordan and was led by the Spirit into the wilderness, where for forty days He was tempted by the devil. He ate nothing during those days, and at the end of them He was hungry. The devil said to Him, "If you are the Son of God, tell this stone to become bread." Jesus answered, "It is written: 'Man shall not live on bread alone.'" Luke 4:1–4*

Jesus is described as full of the Holy Spirit and led by the Spirit into the wilderness. The function of the wilderness has been widely debated, but most agree that it represents a place of testing: the place where one's true colors come out! Here the tempter called into question the need for Jesus to follow the guidance of the Father in all things.

Jesus had the power to make the miracle happen: He was the Son of God. He also had the need for it to happen: He was hungry. Also, the suggestion to make a little bread from stones seems innocent. *You have the power. You have the need. Act on you own behalf and make a meal. Feed yourself!* At first glance it may be hard to see what was at stake here. When we consider the reply of Jesus, more becomes clear.

Jesus referred back the story of the provision of manna in the wilderness. He recounted Moses' admonition that the children of Israel not forget the LORD and His goodness (cf. Deuteronomy 8:3). God caused them to hunger there so that they might learn to trust Him to feed them, not just with physical food but also with His very words. God wanted them to desire His words in their hearts more than food in their stomachs. If they would faithfully seek the former, He would always provide the latter.

God's aim back in the wilderness was to reveal what was in their hearts. That's what seasons of testing reveal. He was asking for their allegiance to Him, to surrender to His guidance and lordship. That's the outcome the LORD wants from all of us. He desired that they not take one step without seeking His face, and He sought to engender in them a heart that followed His commands in total, joyful obedience. All this was wrapped up in this simple command of Moses to remember the LORD. Why do this? Moses said, "Be careful to do this so that you may live" (Deuteronomy 8:1). Life as God intends it is only experienced through obedience.

With this temptation, the tempter seeks to separate Jesus from the Father. Would Jesus exercise His own power and meet His own needs, even for something as basic as feeding Himself? Or would His life and ministry be marked by trust in the Father to meet His needs on the Father's terms? In Matthew's account, Jesus' response contains His answer. He proclaims what will sustain Him throughout His ministry, namely, "every word that comes from the mouth of God" (Matthew 4:4).

In one sense, we learn from this temptation that God always has a bigger story going on than what we can see. The strategy of the enemy is to get us to focus on the immediate, the urgent, and the necessary and to take small matters into our own hands. The temptation is to lose sight of the greater work that is taking place. By missing it we cooperate with the enemy and, more important, exchange dependence on the Father for independent self-reliance.

Turning rocks into bread might have been regarded as a mildly presumptuous move at worst, but the implications run much deeper. God was rewriting history (*or redeeming history!*) in the life, death, and resurrection of His Son, Jesus. What was at stake wasn't just a minor lapse of trust in a moment of physical need but the compromise of the redemption story. Satan wanted Jesus to focus on the immediate in the physical realm, but the reply of Jesus brings the bigger story into view.

By rejecting this temptation, Jesus confronts a worldly value and replaces it with a kingdom ethic. He rejects the proposition that we were created as independent entities that thrive and succeed best when we seize for ourselves the greatest possible level of control of our life.

## Personal Application

The decision to resist the temptation of control impacts all we think, say, and do. We work tirelessly to remove variables and gain leverage and maneuverability in making decisions. The idea that we would give up control willingly, replacing it with an intentional humility and absolute dependence on a God whom we cannot see is ludicrous alongside our cultural mores. Yet that is the course Jesus charts, and in doing so He ushers in a kingdom value for everyone who would take up their cross and follow Him.

Our society thirsts for self-determination and individual advancement along the common path. Alternatively, Jesus calls us to rest in the Father's care. What will we do? Are we experiencing the liberation of the life of trust?

Others have latched into the freedom through church history, such as Andrew Murray, who noted, "It is because Christians do not know their own relation to God of absolute poverty and helplessness that they have no sense of the need of absolute and unceasing dependence, or the unspeakable blessedness of continual waiting on God."[7] Likewise, Brother Lawrence wrote these encouraging words for you and me:

> We have a God who is infinitely gracious and knows all our wants. I always thought that He would reduce you to extremity. He will come in His own time, and when you least expect it. Hope in Him more than ever; thank Him with me for the favors He does you, particularly for the fortitude and patience which He gives you in your afflictions. It is a plain mark of the care He takes of you. Comfort yourself, then, with Him, and give thanks for all.[8]

These leaders and others have learned what can only be grasped by following the example of Jesus in the face of temptation through Spirit-empowered obedience. In reflecting on this temptation and the posture of others who have chosen the kingdom path, we find at least three insights emerge for us.

First, *the enemy will attack us where we are weakest, most vulnerable, and often where we are not expecting it: in the little things!* The enemy wants us to think we can be both self-reliant and independent in the small stuff. We cannot, and when we compromise our leadership by trying to make things happen in the name of expedience (cf. Saul in 1 Samuel 13:1–15), we fall prey to this. Why? Because the whole of Christian life and leadership is small stuff!

When we rely on ourselves for the small stuff we chart a course for trusting in ourselves with bigger issues too. Once we have taken the reins, we have no other option than to seek to control our destiny. Our quest for delivering results causes us to lose sight of the internal discipline God may desire to work in us, and the external witness He intends to show through us.

Second, *this temptation surfaces when there are opportunities for us to grab control for ourselves.* This plays to our desire to trust in our own efforts, rely on our experience, depend on our wisdom, and forge ahead based on our instincts and best-laid plans. For example, the Apostle Paul could have trusted his own eloquence in his teaching, but he knew if he did, there would be no power in his message (cf. 1 Corinthians 2:1–5).

In falling to this temptation, we are forced into the position of having to create church growth or ministry expansion. We must raise money, deliver numbers, meet deadlines, and exceed goals, all in our own strength. Sound familiar?

A ministry president visited the office of his CFO and noticed the screen saver that flashed messages across his computer monitor. He was shocked to see that his CFO had keyed in the phrase, "If it's to be, it's up to me!" That motto characterizes the thinking among far too many ministry leaders. We say we trust in God, but we make decisions and operate according to that screen saver philosophy of self-determination.

Third, *this temptation urges us to focus our attention on immediate needs and lose sight of what God desires for our lives and service.* Do we understand the bigger story that God may be unfolding in our church or ministry? What does God want to teach us that may only be learned through absolute obedience that defies logic and requires our surrender to achieve? What can God do only through such allegiance to Him and Him alone?

God calls us to a humble posture because He knows it is the training ground for His greater purposes (cf. 1 Peter 5:5–11). What we forfeit in our penchant for control is engagement with His bigger story. We cease participating with God in His work. We focus on the stones to meet our urgent needs and miss the redemption story that God wants to unfold in us and among those we serve. This story unfolds only by trusting and obeying.

These three kingdom values—focusing on obedience in the little things, trusting in God rather than taking control, and waiting on the Lord's bigger picture to unfold—call us to a place of continually seeking the Spirit's leading and following His guidance even when it feels like that is the last thing we should do. Let's face it—the world rewards bread makers, but the kingdom of God is not built by them but by those who rely solely on the precious words of God.

## Implications for Leadership and Service

Which set of values is driving our leadership and service? We stated at the outset that our definition of success sends us down one of two paths. Let's consider that in light of this first temptation.

When we take the common path and define success in terms of expansion, we lock ourselves into an agenda. For most of us in ministry, it would be terribly hard to consider that God's will is anything else but growth. Strategic planning becomes shaped by this underlying presupposition so that it only seeks to answer the question, "How would God have us grow?" rather than choosing to follow the obedience path, whence we ask, "What does it look like for us to faithfully follow Christ?"

The drive to make growth happen also creates a culture that is ripe for ethical compromise. *When our work is driven by earthly oriented metrics and our employment is determined by production-focused assessments, we will frequently be tempted to do the expedient rather than the obedient.* Consequently, we may also use secular fundraising techniques even if they rub against our values in order to take control and raise the resources we think we need to fuel our expansion.

We may be tempted to employ secular standards of financial management to deliver the expected return for our growth strategies. We may also be lured to compromise our communications, water down our witness, shrink back from taking stands on explosive issues, and tolerate "mission creep" in the pursuit of achieving specific ends. The kingdom path seeks to guard against such destructive drift.

Finally, we may be tempted to use (or even exploit) God's assets in a utilitarian way. We ask only how human and financial resources will help us accomplish our goals rather than how we might better carry out our stewarding responsibilities in relationship to them.

### Relinquish Control: Obedience and Strategic Planning

Let's consider briefly the relationship between obedience and strategic planning and the temptation to take control. When we follow the common path, we take control, trust ourselves to provide, and enact strategies to try to make things happen. We come up with our own big, hairy, audacious targets and expect God to bless and fund them. However, just because a goal is so big it can only be accomplished if God shows up does not mean it aligns with His will.

Alternatively, steward leaders with the kingdom mindset follow God's leading and seek to discern God's will tied to what God has provided. They follow group discernment processes suggested by Ruth Haley Barton and others realizing that strategizing in leadership does not follow a set plan, but rather, is constantly changing.[9]

This explains why strategies must always be linked to faithfulness to the teachings of Jesus. Any adaptability in our leadership is linked to our flexibility to find contentment and be productive with what God has given us, rather than to constantly focus on what we believe we still need.

## The Choice

Are there areas where we are making bread from stones at our church or ministry? Do we forge ahead with our plans and undertake our work without the Spirit's direction? What would it mean for us to live solely on "every word that comes from the mouth of God"? Can we identify any areas where we have taken control? How have our decisions caused us to disengage from God's greater work?

This may sound harsh, but we are exhorting Christ-followers engaged in ministry to examine themselves and see how the temptation of control linked to the pursuit of ends may be contributing to earthly results rather than kingdom outcomes God desires to produce through our obedience.

In chapter six we go into more detail on what we think the obedience path looks like, and in chapter seven we provide readers with practical resources for pursuing kingdom outcomes. For now, we want to expose the link between defining success in terms of church growth and ministry expansion along the common path and the temptations each of us as Christ-followers faces at this first level. If leaders respond with repentance and humility, we can begin to help our churches and ministries abandon allegiance to this dangerous definition and identify those places where it has opened the door for a compromise of our values and short-circuited our kingdom service.

Are we all willing to make the choice to walk the kingdom path? To relinquish control and humbly serve, relying on "every word that comes from the mouth of God" requires absolute surrender. Henry Blackaby aptly summed up this perspective:

Absolute surrender involves giving up our desires, goals and preferences to God and accepting God's will, regardless of how difficult it may be. Another adjustment we must make to do God's will is reaching a place of total dependence on God. Jesus said, "You can do nothing without Me" (John 15:5). As God's servants we must be in that intimate relationship so He will complete His work through us. We must depend on God alone. When we surrender our lives completely, we become totally dependent on Him, then we understand that, apart from Him, we can do nothing. We must learn to live in constant awareness of our absolute reliance on God if He is to accomplish His purposes through us. This adjustment requires a shift from doing good work for God according to our abilities, gifts, goals, likes, and dislikes to being totally dependent on God, His working, and His resources. It requires courage and faith.[10]

## Chapter Four

# All This I Will Give You: The Temptation of Idolatry

*The devil led [Jesus] up to a high place and showed Him in an instant all the kingdoms of the world. And he said to Him, "I will give you all their authority and splendor; it has been given to me, and I can give it to anyone I want to. If you worship me, it will all be yours." Jesus answered, "It is written: 'Worship the Lord your God and serve Him only.'"* Luke 4:5–8

This scene marks the second temptation. Notice the shift in the setting of the text. The location has changed from the wilderness, a place of testing, to a high place.

In biblical times, the high places were the locations where allegiances were declared and where altars were set up to various gods. Leaders of both Israel and Judah who served God with their whole heart removed all other altars. Leaders who didn't, hedged their bets by honoring God and setting up altars to other gods in the high places. These other altars represent their safety nets in case God did not come through for them.

In this high place, the devil tests the allegiance of Jesus. The devil proclaims that he owns the kingdoms of the earth and can give them to Jesus if He will only bow and worship him. The enemy uses owner language. At the center of this temptation is the renunciation of a truth evident throughout Scripture: God owns everything! Like a snake oil salesman, the tempter offers something he cannot deliver using the language of possession and power. The price tag is worship and service. Satan asks Jesus to give him worship and service in this high place.

Because Jesus was fully man, He could have been tempted to grasp at these things and the security they allege. But He was not fooled. He saw through the devil's lie. In Matthew's account of this scene, His reply employed strong rebuke language: "Away from me, Satan! For it is written, 'Worship the Lord your God and serve Him only.'" Perhaps the reply of Jesus was so sharp because the idolatry of ownership—that is, placing trust in what we can see—may be the greatest temptation we will face as steward leaders. It taps into our fallen nature that desires to possess for ourselves and keep from others. This also leads us to serve the wrong master. Consider the words of Jesus in Luke 16:10–15:

> *Whoever can be trusted with very little can also be trusted with much, and whoever is dishonest with very little will also be dishonest with much. So if you have not been trustworthy in handling worldly wealth, who will trust you with true riches? And if you have not been trustworthy with someone else's property, who will give you property of your own? "No one can serve two masters. Either you will hate the one and love the other, or you will be devoted to the one and despise the other. You cannot serve both God and money." The Pharisees, who loved money, heard all this and were sneering at Jesus. He said to them, "You are the ones who justify yourselves in the eyes of others, but God knows your hearts. What people value highly is detestable in God's sight."*

Have we been faithful in handling worldly wealth, or do we serve it as our master? What does our behavior demonstrate that we value? Have we been trustworthy to put God's resources to work or have we set up financial safety nets in case God's plan for us differs from our own?

## Personal Application

We draw three insights from the response of Jesus to this temptation and His instruction in this related text for the life of the steward leader. First, *we cannot serve God and money, period!* The idolatry of ownership puts us in bondage. We become enslaved to the things we think we own.

Jesus came to set us free to serve as stewards in the world He owns. We are set free to live and lead with the heart of faithful stewards who understand that everything belongs to God. In this paradigm, God alone receives our worship. Furthermore, our obedience to Him with regard to our relationship to earthly wealth is the decisive factor that determines our possession of true riches.

The second insight is, quite frankly, sobering. *Jesus does not put His trust in what He can see, while the religious leaders do.* The religious leaders in this text, and far too many religious leaders today, are lovers of money. What does that mean? They have bowed their knee to the devil by thinking money will solve the challenges of ministry. This explains why they spent all their time chasing after it. No wonder they are portrayed as plundering widow's houses and parading around in long robes (cf. Mark 12:38-40).

Elsewhere in the New Testament, James spoke out against favoritism in the early church. Why? It is probably because many thought that rich people held the keys to ministry success when Christ alone must be our hope. Are we like the religious leaders and those who showed favoritism to the wealthy betraying that we too are lovers of money?

The third lesson is linked to worship and service. *In the high places of life, has our worship and service shifted to acquiring what we can see rather than trusting God whom we cannot see?* Has our allegiance shifted from God to that which we can possess? Has our security been vested in our endowments rather than in a daily dependence on God to be our Provider? Do we only move ahead when we can see the way and the means clearly for ourselves, or do we trust God and go where and when He calls us?

In response to this temptation, Jesus not only rebuked the devil, He cited the *Shema*, the central teaching in the Old Testament Law that every Jewish boy and girl would have been taught from childhood. In quoting Deuteronomy 6:13, Jesus proclaimed that bowing to the enemy would shift everything. His worship and also His service would be a direct violation of the most basic principle in God's Law. In modern terms, Jesus said: "No way!" But do we?

## Implications for Leadership and Service

Let's examine the connection between this temptation and how we define success. When we take the common path, money is the driving force of ministry. Should it be?

The most nefarious notion that prevails in churches and ministry settings today is that we as leaders often think that money is the main thing we need to make ministry successful. We say things like, "If we only had $50,000, then we could…"

Just like the disciples who thought money was the answer to feeding the five thousand, we turn to money and the power it wields rather than God who provides the money. To say such statements reveals we have succumbed to the temptation of believing we are in control and that we are the owners. God, forgive us and help us get our thinking straight.

We must also check our language. The use of possession language takes us down a slippery slope. Phrases like "our church" or "our ministry" reveal another issue. Such talk leads us to one of the most heinous sins of Christian ministry: instead of loving people and using money, we love money and use people.

When we as leaders see ourselves in control and believe all we need is money and people to produce the outputs and results we desire for "our" ministry, we are standing at the cliff's edge from which we can easily fall. A. W. Tozer called this "the monstrous substitution":

> There is within the human heart a tough, fibrous root of fallen life whose nature is to possess, always to possess. It covets things with a deep and fierce passion...Things have become necessary to us, a development never originally intended. God's gifts now take the place of God, and the whole course of nature is upset by the monstrous substitution.[11]

We commit this substitution when we talk, act, or think as though we own our people, our work, our success, our reputation, our time, and our possessions. In so doing, we become enslaved by them all! This bondage need not be our legacy. It is the antithesis of the life God created us to live. If we want to lead in freedom, we can only find it on the kingdom path fueled by obedience.

When we worship God and serve Him only, we keep ourselves from being enslaved by other masters. As followers we are not driven to possess but to love and serve in accordance with our Master's instructions and at the pace of His provision.

Obedience to God and the alignment of our strategies with Scripture position us for kingdom outcomes, also known as fruit. This does not mean that we won't have difficulties. It simply means that we will not try to use people and money to accomplish our purposes. We will, instead, invite others to participate with us in God's work as faithful stewards and obedient disciples. With this perspective, disciples are blessed, ministry is accomplished, and God gets all the glory. And the people we serve notice when they are treated in this way!

## Rejecting Idols: Obedience and Sustainability

What are we trusting in for sustainability? When our church boards and ministry leadership teams talk about sustainability, we often refer to it as financial sustainability. Does this language reflect idolatrous thinking? We recognize that sustainability can have a positive meaning when it is defined as having adequate reserves to fund restricted projects and known cyclical swings in revenue. These can be proper stewardship practices. However, as we said previously, it becomes idolatrous when sustainability is a synonym for a dependence on money to sustain ministry. Biblically speaking, our fiscal management must aim at doing what is right before God and man (cf. 2 Corinthians 8:21) while maintaining a posture of dependence upon God for all of our provision.

The temptation is ever present to turn to secular fundraising practices, worldly investment plans, and the hoarding of resources under the guise of wise planning. In these high places, we reveal that our trust is not in God alone. Our safety nets demonstrate we have bowed to the enemy and the kingdom he promises to give us.

Do we want the ministry we serve to continue in the days to come? Jesus instructs us to tell God what we need and trust in His provision. We also get to invite God's people to join us in His work and trust Him to move in their hearts. Simultaneously, we need to use wisely what God has given us and be content with it. We must also move courageously into the future to which He is calling us and trust Him to sustain us. All this requires trust.

We learn this in the Sermon on the Mount. Jesus called us to be worry-free people because God's care is so good and trustworthy. He added that "the pagans" worry about what they will eat, drink, and wear (cf. Matthew 6:32). What are we instructed to do if we need something? Jesus tells us to "ask the Father" (cf. Matthew 7:7–11).

Sustainability is not about hoarding wealth to secure our future under the guise of saving but about maintaining a posture of dependence on the Father. Do we exhibit this? Consider again the thoughts of Tozer:

> The man of pseudo faith will fight for his verbal creed but refuse flatly to allow himself to get into a predicament where his future must depend on that creed being true. He always provides himself with secondary ways of escape so he will have a way out if the roof caves in. What we need very badly these days is a company of Christians who are prepared to trust God as completely now as they know they must do at the last day.[12]

The mark of godly leaders is where we place our trust. Is our safety net a stockpile of money or the promises of God?[13] There is no more revealing test of trust than this in the high places of life.

## The Choice

Which path do our actions reveal we are on—the common path or the kingdom path—linked to the temptation of idolatry? What testimony do we proclaim through our worship and service? Walking the kingdom path requires resolve and faith. To stay on course we must remain in step with the Holy Spirit. It may also call us to go against the flow, as Jen Hatmaker recently noted:

> In a culture of hero worship and conspicuous rainmakers, this concept struggles to emerge, but the story of God's people comprises a billion little moments when an average believer pressed on, carried through, stepped up. In the quantity of ordinary obedience, the kingdom truly advances.[14]

Obedience demands the divine fortitude to say no to the temptation to place our trust in anything but God alone, and to say yes instead to trusting and serving God in how we live and lead. St. Augustine exhibited this kind of determination in his life and leadership. He offered us this prayer recorded in one of his letters to a fellow pilgrim. May it encourage each of us to walk the kingdom path:

> Such, O my soul, are the miseries that attend on riches. They are gained with toil and kept with fear. They are enjoyed with danger and lost with grief. It is hard to be saved if we have them; and impossible if we love them; and scarcely can we have them, but we shall love them inordinately. Teach us, O Lord, this difficult lesson: to manage conscientiously the goods we possess and not covetously desire more than you give to us.[15]

# Chapter Five

# Leap of Fame:
# The Temptation of Pride

*The devil led [Jesus] to Jerusalem and had Him stand on the highest point of the temple. "If you are the Son of God," he said, "throw yourself down from here. For it is written: 'He will command His angels concerning you to guard you carefully; they will lift you up in their hands, so that you will not strike your foot against a stone.'" Jesus answered, "It is said: 'Do not put the Lord your God to the test.'" When the devil had finished all this tempting, he left him until an opportune time.* Luke 4:9–13

The location of the temptations has moved from the wilderness to the high place and now to the top of the temple. The context has also shifted from a place of testing to a location for declaring allegiance and now to the pinnacle of the place where God must receive all glory. Here we find the most insidious of all insinuations. Satan tempted Jesus using, of all things, Scripture.

Satan suggested that Jesus should throw himself off with the assurance that the angels will break His fall and escort Him gently to the ground. What a great way for Jesus to start His earthly ministry! This stunt would win Jesus widespread acclaim. After all, He is the Son of God, and the Father did command His angels to watch over Him. Right?

It seems this could help God's overall plan too. No need for muddling along in Galilee from town to town. He could start in Jerusalem, the heart of the city He came to redeem. This was His chance to gain fame, popularity, praise, notoriety, and recognition. Why *not* do it?

Jesus again quoted from Scripture, warning the devil as Moses warned God's people: "Don't put the LORD your God to the test" (Deuteronomy 6:16). If you read further in that text to put it in context, you find, "Do not put the LORD your God to the test as you did at Massah."

What happened in Massah? If you flip back to Exodus 17, you will find God's people were anything but cooperative. They quarreled with Moses and grumbled against God. They whined about wanting to go back to Egypt. In modern language, they wanted things their way rather than God's way.

Had Jesus succumbed to the temptation to draw attention to Himself through a dramatic act, seeking the praise of men, He would have become the focus of our fascination but not the Savior of our souls. Jesus rejected the popularity of the public and refused to fall to the temptation to be lifted up by anyone but God. To fall for this temptation would be to steal glory from God.

Here again we see Jesus reject a cultural value and replace it with a kingdom ethic. Jesus set aside the easy road that is strewn with immediate gratification and personal aggrandizement. He refused to be the focus of the work of God, desiring instead that God alone be lifted up. He lifted up the kingdom values of selflessness, humility, and a driving desire to glorify God in everything.

He became a person of no reputation, not willing to grasp even His own divinity, but He emptied Himself, and He calls His followers to do the same (cf. Philippians 2:1–11). He would have only one source of affirmation, the voice of His heavenly Father. In order to hear that voice, Jesus rejected the desire to pine after any other. His pattern was precise. He would say only what the Father said to say and do only what the Father said to do.

## Personal Application

This final temptation brings three realities into view for each of us. First, *our actions reveal our heart condition.* May our push for producing results reveal an unspoken belief that God desperately needs us? Do we believe that if we don't get bigger and do more each year, somehow God's work will be left undone?

We may not admit this openly, but it comes across in our newsletters, our direct mail appeals, and other communications. Spiritual pride can masquerade under the guise of ministry zeal. Sadly, to justify the thirst for accolades, we can be tempted to do exactly what the devil entices in this text. We can misuse Scripture to rationalize our behavior and manipulate other people.

Second, *to avoid damaging effects of pride, we must see every decision as an opportunity to discern God's agenda for the church or ministry we serve because, after all, it belongs to Him anyway.* Practically speaking, Paul refers to this as praying without ceasing.

How do we respond when we have the opportunity to make a name for ourselves? Do we jump at the chance to gain instant glory for ourselves? Or do we, in a posture of perpetual prayer, discern and resist this temptation? What if we discerned through prayer that we were to shrink the ministry by twenty percent next year? How would our board, staff and ministry partners who give and serve faithfully respond? Or what if we believed God was calling us to step down from our roles without another job?

Are we in a position to hear if God led us in such a manner? Are we, and those with whom we serve, willing to respond in obedience? Our greatest obstacle may very well be corporate pride that refuses to allow our ministries to report anything but success in controlling ends and achieving growth.

Remember, even the disciples of Jesus discussed the notion of making Him king. He had to remind them repeatedly to abandon worldly thinking for a kingdom view that submits to the will of the Father. Similarly, Paul received a message from God instructing him where to minister and where not to minister (Acts 16:7–8). He was in a listening posture and responded obediently. These scenes, along with the temptations, are recorded for us. Will we likewise be obedient?

A third insight we can gain from this temptation is that *God is in control and any other view is driven by pride.* Consider more closely some of the kingdom outcomes of the recent global economic crisis. Many Christian leaders have expressed that while they followed God's leading to decrease in size and budget during the financial collapse, they actually carried out their core mission more effectively.

Others have stated that they eliminated peripheral staff and programs that had been allowed to exist during strong financial years. Some even found new ways of collaborating and sharing resources with other ministries previously considered as competitors. The telling conclusion is that such activity would have been unthinkable had financial exigency not pressed them into it.

It is entirely possible that God may have been leading them in these directions even during their strong years, but it took a crisis to get the attention and action of ministry leaders. Why did it take a financial crisis to bring about changes that resulted in more efficient and effective ministry?

This is about obedience. It is hard to cultivate in a production-driven world where we have become prideful executives who think we control the ends.

## Implications for Leadership and Service

How does this temptation align with our definition of success? We said at the outset that when success is measured in terms of church growth and ministry expansion along the common path, churches and ministries hire production-driven leaders who implement expansion-focused strategies measured by earthly oriented metrics in a culture of results-based management and a utilitarian view of resources. Imagine now embedding an allegiance to position, praise, and applause in the mix. It's a recipe for disaster!

The ethics of the world promote competition as a goad to better performance. Such thinking rewards efforts with accolades and renown. This is a primary driver along the common path. How much of our drive for expansion is really seated in the prideful desire to become bigger, more financially stable and prominent than other churches in our community or ministries in our sector?

Recently a pastor suggested that if churches just hit a certain attendance figure, then they would be sustainable. He also offered what he expressed were the proven tactics to grow a church to that size. Likewise, a Christian university leader noted that her school had spent a decade developing a formula. Those who use it can expect to attain certain enrollment targets and institutional rankings nationwide.

Do these perspectives reflect a drive to produce results or a posture of obedience? Again we must clarify that growth is not the issue. The mindset we are warning against is that of a desire for expansion that can become the driving force for ministry. When this happens, pride is the root of the problem.

Consider these questions: What (or who) determines our identity in this life? Does our position, and the prestige and power it holds, determine our identity? Is our financial status and what money can buy the basis of our identity? Or do we associate our identity with our performance and the praise it brings us? As Christ-followers we are tested daily with these and other questions. How do we respond?

We can ask the same questions of the ministries we serve. How prone are we to comparison, asking if we are as large, as financially stable, as fast growing or as well known as another ministry? Whose affirmation are we seeking with such statements? Do we focus on the prominence of our church or ministry rather than the prominence of God in all we do?

We believe that misplaced identities are a major source of leadership and ministry failure. When we yield to the temptation to prop up our reputation, promote our plans, and pursue worldly applause, we may be finished as effective leaders in God's kingdom. Our actions reveal we may be on the path to disaster, like Moses was when he was disqualified for choosing his way over God's way in Numbers 20.

As followers of Jesus, our identity can be found in only one place— our status as children of God, saved by grace and loved by the Creator of the universe. God alone promises to lift us up, but only if we humble ourselves and serve Him in obedience.

## The Choice

There is a malady that afflicts pastors and ministry leaders. Most all would admit to it but few would associate it with the sin of yielding to this temptation. It looks like this. Production-driven leaders are, by nature, hard workers, even workaholics. The members of their board expects them to control ends and report positive numbers. As such they drive themselves by adopting overwhelming work schedules that demand they work long hours at the cost of family and health. Some even brag about not stopping to rest or exercise.

We've all been guilty of this. We have taken pride in busy schedules with little margin for God. And we have expected our team members to do the same. We don't necessarily dictate this, and we don't have to. All this can be traced to making the choice to follow the common path. We take pride in our production. When we need to succeed for the good of the ministry and the sake of our own reputations, we wreak havoc on our families and the people with whom we serve.

Whether through pride or fear, we are *doing* ourselves to death. Yet we know that whatever work God calls us to do, He does so with the expectation that we can carry out that work with excellence within a time commitment that will not detract from a balanced and healthy life. When we allow our relationships to become unhealthy, we cease doing God's will, no matter how much fruit appears (cf. Matthew 11:28–30; Mark 6:31). That is a sobering reality for many, perhaps most of us.

Hudson Taylor suggests that our failure to trust in God's goodness and wait on Him in this critical area of temptation may actually be the primary contributor to the lack of fruitfulness in many ministries today:

> Since the days of Pentecost, has the whole church ever put aside every other work and waited upon Him for ten days, that the Spirit's power might be manifested? We give too much attention to method and machinery and resources, and too little to the source of power."[16]

Could our prideful self-perception be our greatest limiting factor (cf. James 4:4–10)? Are we our own worst enemy?

There is profound freedom and peace in entrusting the future to the Father rather than trying to control our destiny and tie our self-worth to our production. This frees us to listen and help others listen to God and respond without fear, regardless of how He directs. In so doing, we reject the temptation to be spectacular; instead, we serve with peace, passion and humility.

This is where we must make the choice. As Christ-followers we must tap into this power and operate from this personal position of freedom. How do we accomplish such a task? It starts with standing up to the test like Jesus did, resisting the temptation of pride and fame. We must do this in every circumstance, in every moment of every day.

This may require us to speak the truth into our culture from a position that exhibits a healthy lack of concern about what people may think or who may choose to leave the pews as a result. If we stop counting dollars in our bank account, attendance in our classrooms, and bodies in our pews as signs of success, we have taken a step down the right path of thirsting after obedience and faithfulness as our driving passion.

# Chapter Six

# Following Christ: Ten Marks of Christ-Centered Ministry

*Today we obtained, without any trouble, through the kind hand of God, very suitable premises for the Infant Orphan-House. If we had laid out many hundreds in building a house, we could scarcely have built one more suitable for the purpose. How evident is the hand of God in all these matters. How important to leave our concerns, great and small, with Him; for He arranges all things well! If our work be His work, we shall prosper in it.*[17] George Mueller

This chapter contains ten marks that Christ exhibited in His earthly ministry. Each of the ten can be traced in the early church throughout the New Testament. In short, we believe this represents the course Jesus charted for ministry and the path the first disciples trod.

We must consider three assumptions before exploring these ten marks together. First, *any person who desires to follow God and participate with Him in His work must resist the three temptations linked to control, idolatry and pride.* Those who don't will fall into the devil's trap, adopt the world's way of thinking and likely end up like the first century religious leaders: proud, controlling lovers of money.

Our prayer is that so far this study has prompted self-examination and, where needed, repentance and resolve to define success in kingdom terms rather than along the common path.

Second, *these ten traits are formational, not formulaic.* They are neither a checklist of things to acquire, nor a magic formula for ministry success. That means they are descriptive, not prescriptive. They mark the path of Jesus, which is vital for each of us to understand, especially in light of His all-encompassing imperative: "Follow me." Because following is a process, we suggest formational practices with each of the ten traits for growing in Christ-centeredness. These are practical suggestions for discerning how to stay on the kingdom path.

Third, *these biblical characteristics are written for Christ-followers.* As such, they are not our ideas but biblical ones. They are God's instructions, which will appear as foolishness to the world. That's okay with us. We did not author this book for the world. There are plenty of books for thinkers who define success in terms of growth and expansion.

This book is for followers of Jesus who want (in the words of George Mueller that opened this chapter) nothing more than their work to be His work. Mother Teresa also shared this view. "Who can outdo God in His generosity: if we poor human beings give Him everything and surrender our whole being to His service? He is sure to stand by us and with us, as everything in us will be His."[18] When our work is His work through us done in His way, the results will be kingdom outcomes.

We propose ten marks, two for each of the five facets of the kingdom path. We believe they point the way for each of us—whether we are pastors or parishioners, executives or employees—who engage in God's work and desire to pursue kingdom outcomes.

| Following Christ: Ten Marks of Christ-Centered Ministry | |
|---|---|
| Steward Leadership | (1) Submission to the Father<br>(2) Filled, Led and Empowered by the Holy Spirit |
| Faithfulness-Focused Strategies | (3) Prayerful Strategic Planning<br>(4) Raising Kingdom Resources |
| Eternity-Oriented Metrics | (5) Ministry Accountability<br>(6) Transparent Financial Administration |
| Relationship-Based Management | (7) Serving People Humbly<br>(8) Doing Everything with Love |
| Stewardship View of Resources | (9) Mobilizing Spiritually Gifted People<br>(10) Radical Christian Generosity |

Regardless of the path others take, follow Christ with us with the zeal of Jonathan Edwards, whose Seventy Resolutions are summarized as follows: "Resolution One: I will live for God. Resolution Two: If no one else does, I still will."[19] And together may God spark another Great Awakening as a result.

## STEWARD LEADERSHIP

The first two marks exhibited by Christ and followed by the first disciples provide us with the proverbial operating system for steward leadership. It starts with submission to the Father. That encompasses everything we think, say, and do. From there, our steward leadership must be filled, led, and empowered by the Holy

Spirit. With each mark, we offer suggestions for growth and application.

## Mark #1: Submission to the Father

Jesus modeled submission in His relationship to the Father. He desired only to say what the Father said to say and do what the Father said to do. He proclaimed in John 5:19, "The Son can do nothing by himself; He can do only what He sees his Father doing, because whatever the Father does the Son also does." Moreover, in John 5:30 He states His central ministry focus: to do the will of the Father.

How did Jesus maintain this submissive posture? He would slip away from people for solitary prayer with the Father (cf. Mark 1:35). His example demonstrates that prayer precedes action or activity. Later, the early church leaders follow the same pattern.

In Acts 6:4 the disciples reveal their devotion to prayer and the Word. Despite the demands linked to the exponential growth of the church, they refused to allow any other activity to supplant those sacred disciplines. Not only was Jesus submitted to the Father, the disciples were too! They adopted the rhythms of Jesus and imitated His Father-centeredness.

What about us? What does submission look like in our lives and ministry? Who drives everything? If it isn't the Father, then we are enslaved to whatever it is.

Submission to the Father is not a one-time exercise but a constant, active process of discerning God's will and doing it regardless of the cost. Dietrich Bonhoeffer reminds us, "When Christ calls a man, He bids him come and die."[20] So we too must die to our own ambitions and prideful desires both personally and professionally.

*Personally, do we carve out time with the Father? Or are our lives so driven by the pressure to perform and produce results that there is little time left for God?* It is interesting to note that in the ministry of both Jesus and the early church, prayer is a priority. Is it so with us? What evidence supports this in our lives?

Additionally, are we spending time in God's Word? This is not about simply gaining knowledge but rather about knowing God and reflecting His love as John Milton noted. "The end of all learning is to know God, and out of that knowledge to love and imitate Him."[21] Do we take the time to allow God's Word to transform us so that our lives exhibit the submissive life that Christ modeled for us?

*Professionally, does the Father dictate our ministry direction or are "sacred cows" in charge?* We all have had them, and we all must slay them! These are the cultural norms or unquestioned practices that dictate behavior and often lock our churches and ministries into patterns of dysfunction rather than obedience.

The opposite of submission to sacred cows is open communication and complete transparency. When our leadership teams are submitted to the Father we have nothing to hide. If, however, there is anything we don't want the public to know or if there is something we'd be afraid to see on the nightly news that may bring dishonor to the Father, then we are harboring dangerous goods. Such things are not in submission.

Sadly, many ministries tolerate borderline or unethical internal practices that are not beyond reproach (cf. 1 Timothy 3:1–7; Titus 1:5–9). Furthermore, they are rationalized as acceptable because they are being performed in the name of Jesus. It's like rationalizing speeding to deliver food to the hungry or theft to share with a person in need. Submission to the Father has no place for secret sin or compromise. This is an all-or-nothing call to obedience. No exceptions.

**Learning the Posture of Submission**

What disciplines do we practice to maintain a perpetual posture of submission to the Father? What is the role of prayer and Bible study with our leadership teams? We offer three suggestions at this stage for getting on track and staying on track.

(1) *Make solitary prayer a priority.* This may mean carving out thirty minutes or an hour each day at home or the office. It might entail having a "God list" of specific petitions in staff meetings. What's on a God list? Whatever results that we cannot control (and don't want to because we would likely mess things up). It could also take the form of a quiet day each month to eliminate noise and distraction in order to commune with God. Whatever rhythms we choose, we must stick with them and make them community disciplines. This runs counter to our busy schedules and ministry cultures driven to make things happen. Let us make prayer a priority so that our talk of submission is more than lip service.

(2) *Determine the role God's Word will play in our lives and leadership.* This is not about reading through a chapter a day so we can check it off our to-do lists. It's about knowing the Scriptures like a bank teller knows authentic $100 bills. Seasoned tellers examine them daily so they know real ones from counterfeits. As God's Word is living and active (cf. Hebrews 4:12), do we read it daily from a posture of submission so that it shapes and influences everything we do (cf. Acts 6:4)? Or do we use God's Word to justify our behavior or leadership decisions in a manner that reflects our personal or organizational agenda to achieve growth and expansion?

(3) *Believe that God will speak, guide, and provide.* So much of our activity in seeking after God is unilateral and self-centered

rather than in submission to the Father. God, forgive us. We pray and often don't anticipate a response (cf. James 1:6–8). We open biblical texts for what we want to find rather than what God may want to teach us. We are self-centered. We ask God to provide and don't give space for His response. Then we demonstrate a lack of trust with our backup plans. This is not about exhibiting false humility. The serenity of quietness and trust cannot be faked; it's forged on the anvil of submission.

## Mark #2: Filled, Led, and Empowered by the Holy Spirit

In Luke 4:1 we see Jesus portrayed as full of the Holy Spirit, and led by the Spirit. Then after His victories over the devil, His ministry commences in the power of the Spirit (cf. Luke 4:14). The Holy Spirit filled, led, and empowered the ministry of Jesus.

Near the end of His earthly ministry, Jesus told the disciples that He would pray and ask the Father to send the Holy Spirit to teach them all things and help them remember all He taught them (cf. John 14:25). What a gift! It's so amazing that John Chrysostom, an early church leader, proclaimed, "God has given us the greatest gift possible and in profusion...What is this gift? It is the Holy Spirit!"[22] Do we share this enthusiasm?

When the Holy Spirit arrived in Acts 2, the scene is described as having more special effects than a sci-fi movie and more action than an epic thriller. God's presence filled the place. A sound like that of a mighty wind blew through the room where they were gathered, and tongues of fire rested on them. At once they began to speak in the languages of the nations of the ancient world. Why is this significant?

Jesus had just told them in Acts 1:8 that they would receive power with the coming of the Holy Spirit and that they would be His witnesses in Jerusalem, Judea, and Samaria and to the end of the earth. Jesus not only told His disciples the ministry they would have, He provided the power for ministry through the Holy Spirit.

As ministry grew in the early church, things grew larger than the disciples could handle. Co-workers who were "full of faith and the Holy Spirit" were appointed (Acts 6:5). A simple reading of Acts of the Apostles reveals that it is not the work of people but the power of the Holy Spirit that is the leading force in mission. Throughout the rest of the New Testament, Christ-followers are filled, led, and strengthened by the Holy Spirit.

Severian of Gabala, another early church father, noted, "The Spirit in us tends toward fellowship with God. He gives us ever more grace and turns us away from the love of the world."[23] Is the Spirit filling, leading, and empowering us by grace today? If so, is there evidence to validate this in the form of growing godliness and decreasing worldliness? We suggest these three traits indicate Spirit-filled, led, and empowered ministry.

(1)  Spirit-filled Christ-followers position themselves for God's presence in their lives. Saints through the centuries have emphasized that Christians must neither minister out of human strength and wisdom, nor love out of our own capacities and power. We are, rather, to put ourselves in a place where we are constantly being filled by the fullness of God's Spirit so that we can perpetually empty ourselves in service to others following the example of Jesus (cf. Philippians 2:5–11). Do our schedules and lives show we are doing this?

(2)  Spirit-led Christ-followers depend on hearing God speak. Are we a listening culture focused on obedience to what we hear? Is this evident in our meeting and retreat agendas? What

discernment processes and margin for discussion and listening are in place? To experience the unity of the Spirit, are we allotting time to share how God may be speaking to us? A review of our agendas may reveal that we are doing most or all of the talking. It may be time for us to allot space for hearing God together. Would those inside and outside our ministry describe our leadership teams as led by the Holy Spirit?

(3) Spirit-empowered Christ-followers move in response to the Spirit's guidance. As many board and leadership agendas are focused on controlling ends and delivering results, might we be excluding room for following the Spirit to guide and empower us altogether? Early church meetings like the Jerusalem Council of Acts 15 certainly reflect such capacity. In what may be the first set of board minutes on record, the council letter in Acts 15:23–29, the text notes that the result of the meeting "seemed good to the Holy Spirit and to us." The Jerusalem Council's decision-making process reveals the guidance of the Spirit and obedient movement in response. Do our meetings reflect the same?

Remember Paul and Barnabas were to take the gospel to the Jews. Had their ministry been measured by earthly oriented metrics, they likely would have been fired at the Jerusalem Council. Furthermore, with Gentiles coming to faith, they could have been disciplined for violating ends-focused policies that are prevalent along the common path.

If our leadership teams are not filled, led, and empowered by the Holy Spirit, then we are leading in place of the Holy Spirit. No wonder we have the proclivity to lean toward worldliness over godliness. We posture to take control and lead by our own human reason. Paul spoke of this tendency in his letter to the Galatians (3:3):

"Are you so foolish? After beginning by means of the Spirit, are you now trying to finish by means of the flesh?" Functioning by way of the Spirit clashes with modern-day secular thinking and the prevailing patterns and practices along the common path. To do this requires us to exchange our will for God's will.

John MacArthur gives helpful insight into how we can understand God's will in light of the New Testament. God's will is that we are saved (cf. 2 Peter 3:9), sanctified (cf. 1 Thessalonians 4:3), filled with the Spirit (cf. Ephesians 5:18), submissive (cf. James 4:7), and that along with Him (most people want to forget this one) we endure suffering (cf. 1 Peter 2:21).[24] Before embarking on a ministry career, we must each ask ourselves this question: Am I willing to exchange my own will for His will?

### Yielding to the Holy Spirit

There are many ideas for growing in this area. We offer two practical suggestions to help steward leaders to yield to the Holy Spirit, to ensure all ministry is filled, led, and empowered by God within us.

(1) *Practice the inward disciplines of meditation and fasting to nurture your spiritual life.*[25] Meditation is about hearing and obeying God's Word. We must look intently into the Scriptures and take time to consider the practical implications of what we are reading (cf. James 1:22–25). This exercise will cause us to live very differently from the world around us. We advise you to get some rest before you do this. Many spiritual directors, like Jenni Hoag, have attested that a great hindrance to our spiritual growth is exhaustion.[26] We must be rested to sit quietly and meditate on the ways the Spirit may be seeking to minister to and speak to us through time spent in God's Word.

Regarding fasting, choose a time on a regular basis to forgo food and drink for the purpose of drawing near to God. Such behavior does not win us favor before God. We fast not for God but for ourselves. In fasting we set aside all other appetites to feast on and be filled with the Bread of Life. Research reveals that fasting was a key contributor to the Great Awakening in the late 1700s and early 1800s. If we want to see another one, let's fast and call God's people to join us and pray for God to pour out His Spirit. Revival just might break out!

These inward disciplines precede any outward movement. Only after taking the inward journey, by way of prayer, study, meditation, and fasting, are we in a position to be filled, led, and empowered by the Holy Spirit.

(2) *Inspect people for fruit rather than evaluating performance.* Are the fruit of the Spirit evident in our lives and our team members' lives (cf. Galatians 5:22–23)? We should look for fruit as an indicator of the Spirit-filled, led, and empowered life (cf. 1 Corinthians 5:12). This represents a shift from modern convention, where performance evaluations are often tied to results that we (and our staff members) may not be able to control. Instead, we suggest that any assessment should be linked to faithfulness to duties we can control and assessment of fruit evident from the perspective of managers and co-workers. Sound too radical? Some leaders are choosing this path, though it goes against the flow.

One national ministry recently took the bold step to engender a steward leader culture rooted in these ideas. Some might label them foolish (in their thinking) as the step shifts the focus of evaluation from earthly oriented metrics that are prevalent along the common path to eternity-oriented metrics from the kingdom path. We celebrate their resolve to resist cultural pressures. This ministry is positioned for fruitfulness linked to obedience.

In another ministry, each supervisor asks direct subordinates (annually in one-on-one meetings) to share fruit they believe God is producing in their lives. Supervisors do this to help staff members focus on their inward spiritual growth as well as their outward professional development. This demonstrates that the ministry values people who endeavor to keep in step with the Spirit as well as grow in their skills and service. Imagine a supervisor who cared more about the condition of each person's soul than the level of that person's production! The outward journey of each staff member at this ministry is positioned for Spirit empowerment rather than flowing from what the flesh can muster.

Fruit that results from this approach include greater productivity, higher morale, and employee satisfaction. These often lead to growth and greater mission impact. Whether the growth happens or not, the fruit represents kingdom outcomes.

## FAITHFULNESS-FOCUSED STRATEGIES

If the first two marks comprise the operating system, these next two provide the applications for us to run. These apps, or strategies, are intended to help us stay focused on faithfulness. They turn our attention to how we approach planning and how we raise kingdom resources. Both seek to ensure that direction and provision are perpetually dependent on God.

## Mark #3: Prayerful Strategic Planning

The plan for the growth of the earthly ministry of Jesus flowed from prayer. Luke 6:12–13 records that Jesus prayed all night, and only after that time of communion with God did He call a large number of disciples to Himself and choose twelve from among them. It seems odd that for ministry to grow He would trim the number of apostles. God-directed planning often seems counterintuitive (cf. Gideon in Judges 6–7).

Likewise in the early church, passages such as Acts 13:1–3 illustrate a similar result. In this scene, five prophets and teachers—Barnabas, Simeon, Lucius, Manaen, and Saul—came together to worship, fast, and pray in Antioch. Commentators believe the ethnic roots of their names suggest that they would have represented the leading people groups in the ancient Mediterranean world.

Had their focus been on producing massive ministry results, they likely would have planned five preaching tours to their respective peoples. In what seems to mirror the Luke 6 account, only after much prayer does the plan surface. The Spirit taps a smaller number of them, Barnabas and Saul, for the work God had prepared for them (cf. Acts 13:3).

Prayerful planning positions steward leaders to know what work God would have them do. It is sometimes the opposite of what the world recommends. We see this throughout Scripture. Often this takes place so that the Spirit of God comes into view as the power of ministry.

Rather than contrive a magic planning formula such as "think small to grow big" from these texts, notice the prayerful planning posture that precedes ministry. People who are gifted for ministry come together in prayer and don't move forward until they receive their marching orders, their plans, from God. If there is a lesson for modern-day leaders, it is to bring people together in prayer and wait for direction.

*Waiting before working is a key theme throughout Scripture and a counterintuitive characteristic of Christ-centered ministry.* Those on the common path operate from a presupposition that expansion and growth are the key determinants of organizational success, so they want to start working yesterday! Strategic planning becomes subservient to predetermined production metrics. Goals reflect different aspects of how the ministry should grow, and annual plans flesh out the steps needed to achieve that growth. Planning meetings may be opened in prayer, but ministry leaders who see the enlargement of their work as the only acceptable future set the direction. We have been guilty of such thinking and have experienced strategy sessions where achieving growth overwhelmed any sense of a quest for an alternative course of action.

Those on the kingdom path see planning in an entirely different light. The leadership team starts by listening openly and intently for the voice and guidance of God through the presence of the Holy Spirit. These people do not proceed until they discern that God's voice has been heard. Once they understand God's vision for their future, strategic planning serves as the tool that assures alignment with this vision. Planning is their stewardship response to the Word of God spoken to them. Having heard where they are to go, they plan strategically how they will get there. Prayer guides this step to ensure that strategies stay consistent with God's instructions. Just as the vision is not theirs, the plan also belongs to God, and the leadership team trusts Him to guide its execution.

How do we approach strategic planning? Can we truly say that our plans are developed in response to the vision God has laid on our hearts? Or do our plans inculcate our own desires to expand our work and our vision based on earthly metrics and assumptions? These are fundamental questions we as leaders must ask ourselves.

## Engaging in Spirit-guided Planning

When leaders engage in prayerful planning as an act of stewardship to ensure obedience to God, planning becomes a spiritual practice. Here is a practical definition of Spirit-guided planning and five considerations for engaging in it. Consider (and feel free to adopt) this definition:

> Prayerful strategic planning is a process of faith that is filled, led and empowered by the Holy Spirit, where we as ministry leaders seek together to hear God's voice and discern His will regarding the future in a way that enables us to pursue kingdom outcomes with organizational passion (unity of vision) and Christ-like excellence (obediently offering our very best).

Once we have defined prayerful strategic planning, we advise leaders to mind five considerations:

(1) *Involve a sampling of stakeholders.* Processes that limit input and rely on a few to make sweeping decisions run the risk of falling back onto personal agendas. This does not mean that we have fifty people at the strategic planning table, but it requires us to invite representatives from our community. This also builds ownership and helps maintain unity in the discernment process. Outside voices also help identify sacred cows and challenge any lack of transparency.

(2) *Plan prayer coverage.* Prayer must be more than a meeting opener. This calls for a coordinated process to prepare the

sampling of stakeholders to hear from God, and to seek collectively, His divine protection and direction. To listen and hear as a community, we need to prepare our hearts and minds. This focus may be encouraged with a centering prayer, which contains a solitary nondirective question, such as, "What would you have for us, Lord?"

(3) *Test your assumptions.* Few things squelch the movement of the Spirit faster than false assumptions. Since prayerful planning maps a forecast of the future, we must come together around facts. Discussing these can be difficult. Just ask the Jerusalem Council (cf. Acts 15)! Many leaders think this bogs down the process; in actuality it helps us as a group to go slow in order to go fast. We believe it is worth the extra time and effort. Ultimately, the tough test modeled by the Jerusalem Council is to filter all we discuss through our knowledge of God's Word and the leading of the Holy Spirit.

(4) *Define objectives according to kingdom values.* Too often our goals seem to be written to meet specific personal or institutional needs and further ministry agendas. Just as our mission statement should be a reflection of our calling to serve God's kingdom, so our strategic plans must do the same. When we read through a ministry's or church's strategic plan, we should be praising God for the kingdom impact it will have, not for the internal capacity or numerical growth it will produce. Although numeric results may come, we must state our objectives in terms of obedience. If we cannot, we need to go back and see where we have missed the mark in our planning process. Again, consider the Jerusalem Council as an example. The result of their planning session was four obedience-oriented parameters that did not seek to control the growth of God's Church but, rather, unleash it (cf. Acts 15:29).

(5) *Build agility into the plan.* No matter how hard we work at gaining stakeholder input, covering the process in prayer, testing assumptions alongside God's Word and the Holy Spirit, and defining objectives according to kingdom values, as humans we may at some point think it is "our job" to take the reins. Even the Apostle Paul had to be open to receiving course corrections from the Holy Spirit regarding the practical execution of the plan to take the gospel to the Gentiles (cf. Acts 16:7). He was open to such change, and we must be too!

## Mark #4 – Raising Kingdom Resources

After Jesus picked twelve disciples and launched His earthly ministry, He oriented them with specific instructions. They were to take nothing with them. No bread, no staff, no extra clothes: nothing! Only by going empty-handed could they learn that money is not the driving force behind ministry—God is. Three passages in Luke illustrate this.

Luke 9:1–6 records that Jesus gave the twelve disciples power and sent them forth to preach. God opened doors for them, guided and supplied. Luke 10:1–24 shares a similar scene but this time with seventy-two disciples. He sent them out, told them to pray for fellow workers, take nothing and share God's peace wherever they went. Again, they returned with a joyous report. In Luke 22:35-38, just prior to His arrest, Jesus paused to remind the disciples with these words:

> *Then Jesus asked them, "When I sent you without purse, bag or sandals, did you lack anything?" "Nothing," they answered. He said to them, "But now if you have a purse, take it, and also a bag; and if you don't have a sword, sell your cloak and buy one. It is written: 'And he was numbered with the transgressors'; and I tell you that this must be fulfilled in me. Yes, what is written*

*about me is reaching its fulfillment." The disciples said, "See, Lord, here are two swords." "That's enough!" He replied.*

Jesus was not saying to take up arms for a crusade, though He was about to be arrested. He was also not calling the disciples to stockpile supplies for a revolution. He was asking them if they remembered the lesson they learned when He sent them out with nothing—that God provided for their needs. In bringing this up, He added additional teaching. Once they understood this, He told them (*and us!*) what to do with all God provides henceforth. Put it to work in the spiritual battle before us.

Did they do it? Did the leaders of the early church trust God to provide? As God provided did they put to work the resources at their disposal? We could cite many positive examples from the New Testament. Among them, Barnabas is noteworthy. His real name was Joseph. He was an encourager so they referred to him as Barnabas, which means "son of encouragement." He was a landowner. To own land in antiquity was to possess an asset that could generate income and keep its owner from having to do manual labor. In Acts 4:36–37, we read that Barnabas sold a tract of land and placed the money at the apostles' feet. This reflects obedience to the teachings of Jesus and is significant for the early church (*and for us*) for at least three reasons.

(1) *Barnabas could have allowed his land to be worked for the benefit of the community of faith and simultaneously retained ownership of it.* In other words, he could have put the earnings to work for the kingdom rather than the full value of the asset. While such an approach makes earthly sense, such generosity requires no faith and exhibits no sacrifice. The kind of giving Jesus celebrates is always sacrificial, and sacrifice is what Barnabas did! He sacrificed the security of his asset and put it to work. He sold the tract of land.

(2) *The way Barnabas presented his gift tells us a lot about him; he attached no strings to it.* To set the money at the apostles' feet represents humble submission to the leadership of God's Church. Benefaction inscriptions from antiquity reveal that big givers attached strings to their gifts to ensure recognition and perpetual glory for their generosity. Barnabas showed no such motivation.

(3) *Barnabas gave the proceeds to God.* This act would shift a landowner from trusting in his land to trusting in his God. As the story of the early church in Acts unfolds, Barnabas played a key role in the expansion of mission alongside Paul throughout the ancient Mediterranean world. Interestingly, the text does not portray him as a key player because he is loaded with cash and provides funding for everything. He demonstrated leadership through obedience to the apostles' teachings and by giving encouragement to God's people. Wherever he went he strengthened the faith of the lives he touched.

What about us? What are we trusting in to fuel ministry and secure our reputation? Know that we are not the first to wrestle with these questions. Along with missionary Jonathan Goforth, we must first remember, "All the resources of the Godhead are at our disposal."[27] So if we need something, is our first thought to ask God or ask a person? As the latter is idolatrous thinking, might our ministries struggle at times because our actions as leaders demonstrate that we are not trusting God to provide for our needs? Or are we known for trusting God?

Along these lines, Adoniram Judson added, "It is true that we may desire much more. But let us use what we have, and God will give us more."[28] This is not about manipulating God to get what we want. It's about being faithful with what we have and trusting that if we need more, God will supply more. Have we so quickly forgotten that He has supplied everything up until this point! Paradoxically, it is the faithful use of God's provision that can be linked to receiving greater blessings, though it is not a guarantee of such provision (cf. Luke 16:10–14).

Here we simply note that Jesus wanted the disciples to learn to trust God to provide and then put to work whatever God provided. And in the rest of the New Testament, we see God's people doing just that. The real question is, do we?

Our role as leaders today in raising kingdom resources is not to try to provide per se, but to call God's people to put to work whatever they have. That message should ring through our messages and our mail. Our job is not to raise up gifts but rather to exhort people to become givers—to call people to serve as obedient stewards—who are rich toward God.[29] If we think we are the fundraisers, then we are trying to do God's job, as He is our Provider, not us. How we raise kingdom resources says more about the values that drive us than anything else. It reveals where our trust is.

**Strengthening Our Resolve to Trust God to Provide**

Trusting God to provide is the primary faithfulness-focused strategy Jesus gave His followers and us. Here are three activities we can consider for growing in this area.

(1) *We can adopt a rule of life that positions us to depend on God.*[30] Christ-followers like Augustine of Hippo, Patrick of Ireland, Benedict of Nursia, Francis of Assisi, and Teresa of Avila, or in modern times, George Mueller, Andrew Murray, William Carey, Adoniram Judson, and Mother Teresa, testified to the freedom and peace of the life of trust. For

them "the future was as bright as the promises of God" because as ordinary people they were committed to a way of life that placed their trust solely in their extraordinary God. How about us? Might we also need a rule of life to help us stay on the kingdom path?

(2) *We cannot exhort others to trust God to put God's resources to work while trusting God to provide if we are not doing it ourselves.* Many don't realize that prolific preachers like George Whitefield and Charles Spurgeon started and ran orphanages that specifically depended on God's provision for the support of the children. Many have heard the miraculous stories from George Mueller and his Bristol orphanage, but many other ministry leaders share similar testimonies. Their collective testimony states: only after we have put God's provision to work and resolve to trust God to provide can we learn that He is all we have ever needed all along, and only then can we teach others the same course of obedience.

(3) *We may need to change how we view resources and budgets.* Henri Nouwen calls this "being converted in relationship to our needs."[31] For too long in our church boards and ministry leadership teams we have wrongly thought of money as if it can solve every problem and treated the budget as the guiding force of ministry. Budgets are great tools for accounting for revenues and reporting on the faithful use of God's resources. They help us manage the financial side of stewardship. But just as money is not the answer to every problem, our budgets should not make our decisions for us.

We must neither hoard for security nor squander resources with frivolity. Jesus calls disciples to put resources to work and, with the posture of the Lord's Prayer, trust in His ongoing provision. The early church leaders lived this way and so did prominent saints through the century. With God's help, so can we!

This is perhaps the most important area of self-examination and honest reflection in the life of a leader and the organizations and ministries they serve. If our thoughts are ever dominated by money fears and our meetings have shifted from always talking about mission to always talking about money, it is likely that we have shifted from serving God to serving mammon. Jesus wants us to live differently. We get to exhort God's people to put to work the resources He has provided, sacrificially, like Barnabas, while trusting Him to provide.

## ETERNITY-ORIENTED METRICS

Eternity-oriented metrics value what Jesus values and assess work in order to foster faithfulness. The focus is on the qualitative over the quantitative, that is, measuring success in terms of alignment with the instructions of Jesus. A good rule of thumb to be sure our measures are eternity-oriented is to ask this question: Does it measure growth in God's kingdom or our own? Also, remember that the kingdom path sees results as the fruit that God produces. As such, eternity-oriented metrics surface in two areas: ministry accountability and transparent financial administration.

### Mark #5: Ministry Accountability

When Jesus sent the disciples to proclaim the gospel of the kingdom (cf. Luke 9–10), He sent them out two-by-two. Each of the disciples had an accountability partner to maintain alignment with His instructions. They would also have a companion to encourage them, to share their victories, and to urge them to persevere through difficulty. Two-by-two deployment helps us all as disciples stay on the kingdom path. Interestingly, when the disciples returned in pairs lamenting their inability to produce results on all occasions, Jesus pointed them to prayer (cf. Mark 9:29; Matthew 17:21). This illustration reveals who is in control and who is not.

In the early church, mission goes forth with the same accountability measures in place. Paul and Barnabas, two by two, were the key players on the first missionary journey (cf. Acts 13–14). When they appeared before the Jerusalem Council (cf. Acts 15), accountability measures are evident. Paul and Barnabas reported their faithfulness to proclaim the gospel and the results that followed, though the information they shared was quite different from what the Jewish leaders expected. Gentiles were coming to faith.

Coming out of the Jerusalem Council, mission was multiplied as Paul and Silas set out through Syria and Cilicia, and Barnabas took Mark and sailed to Cypress (cf. Acts 15:39–41). Two went by land, and two departed by sea. As ministry grew exponentially, we see continued attentiveness to ministry accountability in the Apostle Paul's letters.

For example, Paul instructed those he mentored to follow in his steps. He urged that leaders exhibit character that was "beyond reproach" and "blameless" (cf. 1 Timothy 3:1–13; Titus 1:6–11). This does not reflect perfection but integrity and consistency. God's leaders must stand the test of public scrutiny and be found blemish-free. We must follow the primary theme of the letters to the churches in the New Testament and teach nothing inconsistent with the sound words of Jesus (cf. 1 Timothy 6:3-4).

*So that our lives stay aligned with kingdom agendas, rather than our own, do we have personal accountability and assessment measurements in place? Do we utilize two-by-two relationships for ministry accountability?* This runs counter to the common path, as church researchers like Gary McIntosh have reported that pastors do not like accountability. Do we voluntarily allow our ministry efforts to be evaluated by insiders and outsiders to ensure consistency with Scripture? Sadly, if numbers are up, other likely more important issues are often of little interest to elder boards and governance committees.

When anyone in a leadership position is given authority without accountability it can lead to disaster, for our flesh tends toward selfish rather than kingdom purposes. When authority without accountability is embedded within our denominational or ecclesiastical structures, they have the tendency toward building earthly kingdoms rather than the eternal one.

Elsewhere, the president of a faith-based organization functioning from the common path perspective was crushing his team under the weight of earthly oriented metrics (quantitative assessments) rather than eternity-oriented ones (qualitative measures). Under the guise of what appeared to be a kingdom metric of winning more souls for Christ, he was losing the respect of his people and discouraging rather than inspiring their faithful service.

**Maintaining Alignment through Qualitative Measures**

We could put forth a host of qualitative measures to apply this principle because ministry settings vary so widely. For this reason, we offer five for consideration and adaptation.

(1) *Identify accountability partners.* Are we meeting regularly to find encouragement and share challenges that may tempt us to stray from the path of obedience? Often we are too busy to make time for this, in which case, we are too busy not to! We must carve out time in the rhythm of our schedules for sharing

what the Spirit is doing as we live and lead in accordance with the teachings of Jesus and to reveal our struggles for encouragement and to nurture perseverance.

(2) *Find a ministry mentor, such as the Apostle Paul was to Timothy.* Such iron-sharpens-iron relationships offer benefits in both directions. We get out of it what we put into it. But don't make it too difficult. Consider setting up a monthly phone call or face-to-face visit to interact and be open to collaborative projects for mutual learning and kingdom benefit.

(3) *Establish ministry structures that share leadership duties, preserve open accountability, and welcome outside scrutiny.* This is easier said than done. Where should we start? Pastors and senior leaders must lead by example. It may require changing policies, organizational charts, and even annual staff evaluation processes. For staff members in subordinate roles, the implementation of accountability measures should correspond to ministry responsibilities and authority.

(4) *Align plans with staff evaluations and assess faithful activity rather than results staff cannot control.* As Jesus called us to make disciples who observe and teach all He commanded (a qualitative measure linked to a directive), not to win a specific number of souls (a hypothetical quantitative measure), we should do likewise. Let us evaluate staff based on faithfulness to follow plans (activity) not just results (productivity).

(5) *Celebrate what we value.* If we value faithful activity, let's honor it. Too often our evaluative processes and community celebrations reflect that we value primarily qualitative results and the people responsible for making them happen. Praise and recognition have their place, but in the end all accolades

for such fruit must be directed heavenward. The key here is to put eternity-oriented metrics in place and acknowledge them appropriately, because what we celebrate communicates what we value.

## Mark #6 – Transparent Financial Administration

Faithful stewardship or administration of financial resources in the economy of God functions according to an alternative economy than that of the prevailing thinking in the economy of this world. Jesus commends faithful stewards for putting God's resources to work, rather than foolishly hoarding them (cf. Matthew 6:19–21; 25:14–30; Luke 22:35–38), though our culture calls people wise who stockpile for security. He models enjoyment in community and shuns self-centered indulgence (cf. Luke 7:34; 12:13–21), while our culture refers to such luxuries as entitlements.

Transparency is also vital as Jesus urges that we guard from justifying behavior because it is acceptable to man when it is unacceptable before God; for with obedience often comes blessing, and the proclivity of the human heart is to worship provision rather than our Provider—to serve mammon rather than God (cf. Luke 16:10–15). We have record that ordinary people supported the ministry of Jesus financially (cf. Luke 8:1–3). What happened with the money they gave? Judas was the keeper of the common purse, and John 12:6 reveals: *He used to help himself to what was put into it.* It's not surprising that greed would later lead him to betray Jesus for thirty pieces of silver (cf. Matthew 26:15).

*Financial controls in the New Testament helped early church leaders avoid thievery.* For example, in his Corinthian correspondence, Paul expressed a willingness to send faithful couriers to carry gifts or even assist in the effort himself (cf. 1 Corinthians 16:1–4). In his second letter to them, he added this statement regarding the administration of their gift for the needy in Jerusalem (2 Corinthians 8:20–21): "We want to avoid any criticism of the way we administer this liberal gift. For we are taking pains to do what is right, not only in the eyes of the Lord but also in the eyes of man." Paul did not want misappropriation of funds or embezzlement to shame the name of Christ or to discourage Christian generosity.

*Do our ministries put God's resources to work in keeping with the explicit instructions of Jesus, or do our financial decisions reflect the prevailing cultural norms?* The common path practice of storing up money for a rainy day or to guard against decreases in the market or other exigencies directly contradicts the teachings of Jesus. We face a significant challenge to put God's resources to work wisely and carefully without falling into the temptation to let financial resources take the place of God as the source of our security. Remember, our hearts always follow where we put God's treasure.

*Additionally, how attentive are our ministries to matters of financial administration?* What controls are in place for the handling of funds on a day-to-day basis? How many people are involved in those processes so that no one is tempted to help himself or herself to God's resources, like Judas did? Ultimately, attention to this area is about establishing systems that protect our people from temptation and preserve God's reputation.

John Wesley captures this dynamic, which reinforces the importance of having transparent financial administration. When we are obedient, God often blesses in material ways. If we follow the common path, financial blessings will destroy us. Only through faithfulness to follow the kingdom path can we avoid worldliness and continue to participate in God's work.

I fear, wherever riches have increased, the essence of religion has decreased in the same proportion. Therefore do I not see how it is possible, in the nature of things, for any revival of true religion to continue long. For religion must necessarily produce both industry and frugality, and these cannot but produce riches. But as riches increase, so will pride, anger, and love of the world in all its branches.[32]

**Putting Resources to Work and Controls in Place**

We believe there are at least four things that Christ-followers should do with regard to transparent financial administration. These are critical eternity-oriented metrics because they help keep our churches and ministries faithful in handling God's resources, which positions us for fruitfulness.

(1) *Establish biblical principles related to resources before you possess them.* What would we do if someone gave a car, a house, or a million dollars to the ministry? Do we have gift acceptance policies in place? As riches increase thanks to God's generous provision, do we have asset management policies in place for putting those resources to work?

(2) *Implement financial controls.* No one person should count the offering in church or handle money at a ministry without appropriate processes to avoid theft or embezzlement. This will require staff or volunteers with accounting skills who are willing to follow documented procedures. With increasing levels of support received in a digital form, the application of special procedures is necessary to ensure the integrity of these funds.

(3) *Engage an independent certified public accounting (CPA) firm to perform appropriate services.* Even small organizations

may wisely utilize a CPA to compile or review annual financial statements and/or perform other engagements. As ministries grow, CPAs are often engaged to perform an annual financial audit. While audits are not inexpensive, they help ensure that financial data is properly presented and that controls and processes are in place to account for resources in a manner that is right before God and man.

(4) *Submit willingly to the annual scrutiny of an external accreditation organization such as ECFA (www.ECFA.org).* Adherence to ECFA's high standards of integrity in the areas of governance, financial management and stewardship will enhance the trust of your organization with your constituents. Plus, ECFA will help you keep up-to-date on frequently changing laws and regulations, which can be both confusing and cumbersome.

While these suggestions sound expensive, the benefits far outweigh the costs. The cost of CPA services and the annual membership fees to the ECFA are small compared to the confidence these commitments give to the constituents served. Furthermore, it is very difficult to bounce back from having a reputation for financial mismanagement. Remember, the ministries we serve are not ours, they are God's, and it is His name that we steward as we participate with Him in His work.

## RELATIONSHIP-BASED MANAGEMENT

How leaders treat staff in churches and ministries must be different from the world. There are two main descriptors that Jesus uses that comprise relationship-based management: service and love.

## Mark #7: Serving People Humbly

The world sees leadership as desirable because of the power associated with position. Jesus declares disciples who chart a different course as great. In Luke 22:24–27, Jesus declares disciples who chart a different course as great:

> *A dispute also arose among them as to which of them was considered to be greatest. Jesus said to them, "The kings of the Gentiles lord it over them; and those who exercise authority over them call themselves Benefactors. But you are not to be like that. Instead, the greatest among you should be like the youngest, and the one who rules like the one who serves. For who is greater, the one who is at the table or the one who serves? Is it not the one who is at the table? But I am among you as one who serves.*

Jesus modeled humble service for us in His earthly ministry. He exchanged the benefactor (glory-seeking) model for a servant's model. If you want to be great in His kingdom, learn to be a servant of all. At every turn He did not seek to amass power but to give it away!

That's the opposite of how things worked in the world of the New Testament. Because land ownership was a requirement for civic leadership in the cities of the Roman Empire, the rich landowners were trained to function by way of the benefactor model. Patron lords would extend benefactions to clients only as long as they rendered service in return. The rich made the rules that dictated relationships.

The leaders of the early church battled with this prevailing cultural thinking as well. James 2 reveals that favoritism was a real problem in the Jerusalem congregation. The rich were receiving special treatment as compared to that given to the poor. This always leads to disaster in the community of faith because inevitably, people get trampled. Peter exhorted leaders against this too, urging them not to "lord over" those in their care, but to serve as examples to them (cf. 1 Peter 5:3). Paul concurred, calling followers of Christ to take the form of a servant (cf. Philippians 2:1–11).

*Relationship-based management, where leadership is focused on service, ran contrary to social norms in antiquity and looks different today.* The function of management is not to guarantee results as declared by those who follow the common path to success. Instead, we get to serve everyone by teaching them what Christ commanded and by equipping them for works of service (cf. Ephesians 4:11–12).

Steward leaders understand that everyone whom they serve is on a journey of faith. They see these relationships as gifts to steward. They pray that God would work through them to help every employee, colleague, superior, friend and co-worker take the next steps in the journey to becoming more fully the person God created them to be. Steward leaders are set free from focusing on themselves and their personal production, and as a result they lift up everyone around them. Leaders who walk the common path in their work see people as a means to their own ends. Steward leaders who are driven by joyful obedience see people as ends in themselves. In this way, steward leaders incarnate the servant posture of Jesus and manage people through relationships that bear fruit and result in kingdom outcomes.

## Learning to Serve like Jesus

Serving is hard work, and it gets even more difficult as God expands the scope of our leadership. Consider these three ideas for application.

(1) *Start by serving one another.* Bearing one another's burdens and caring for brothers and sisters in the community of faith are probably the greatest witness to the world. They also set a good example about what it means to be a Christian for all who are watching us. We must not overcomplicate this but, rather, humbly practice it, day after day.

(2) *Watch for signs of power struggles.* Christian leadership is not about selfishly posturing for power by playing political games. It's about serving others selflessly. If power struggles emerge, we must bring them into the light by speaking truthfully about them. Such struggles surface all over the New Testament. It was not about Paul or Apollos in Corinth—it was about Jesus (cf. 1 Corinthians 3:1–9). It was not about Euodia or Syntyche in Philippi—it was about Jesus (cf. Philippians 4:2–3).

(3) *Develop leaders in a downward fashion.* While it is noble to desire leadership roles, we must help emerging leaders understand that the road to leadership is a downward slope of self-denial and humility. Profound ministry starts with doing the mundane with Christ-like joy. In a culture that equates the grasp for power with leadership accomplishment, we need to develop men and women who will take up a towel and bowl and view service in Christ's name as their highest calling.

## Mark #8: Doing Everything with Love

God, who is love, sent His Son to accomplish salvation for mankind motivated by love (cf. John 3:16). When asked the most important thing for people to remember, Jesus proclaimed: "'Love the Lord your God with all your heart and with all your soul and with all your mind and with all your strength.' The second is this: 'Love your neighbor as yourself." There is no commandment greater than these" (Mark 12:30–31).

Plain and simple, our love for God should be demonstrated by love for people (cf. 1 John 4:20). This love does not discriminate between Christians and non-Christians, people of the same ethnicity and people of diverse cultures, people of the same socioeconomic class and people at different levels.

To define "love of neighbor," Jesus told the story of the Good Samaritan (cf. Luke 10:25–37). For Jews, Samaritans would have likely been the last people to whom they would think of extending love. With this parable Jesus taught that our neighbor is anyone in need who comes across our path. Were the disciples in the early church like the religious leaders in the story, too busy to stop to help? Or did they extend care to those in need in a manner that was contrary to cultural norms?

Evidence reveals the early church had a reputation for loving God and loving others. This was probably the case because it's what leaders like Paul instructed: "Do everything in love" (1 Corinthians 16:14). Likewise, Paul urged Timothy to remain in Ephesus despite the heresy and opposition that was present there with a similar aim: "The goal of this command is love, which comes from a pure heart and a good conscience and a sincere faith" (1 Timothy 1:5).

Christ-followers are exhorted throughout the New Testament to demonstrate their love for God by doing good deeds. These ranged from feeding the hungry and aiding widows and orphans to practicing hospitality and sharing with others in need. We are to offer such assistance to those in the community of faith and outsiders as well (cf. Galatians 6:10-11).

What is at stake here? Our tendency along the common path which uses results-based management is to *love money and use people*. On the kingdom path, which is guided by relationship-based management, our aim is to *love people and use money*! Which phrase would people say best describes our lives and service? Do we have a personal reputation like Dorcas in Acts 9:36 for our good deeds and care for the poor, or like Cornelius of Acts 10:2 who feared God and gave generously to the needy? Does our church exhibit Macedonian enthusiasm to help those in need (cf. 2 Corinthians 8:1-6)?

Relationship-based management requires us to travel with people on the journey of life. To love our neighbor is to be present with them in good times and bad. It means placing the needs and goals of our neighbor above our own. It entails setting aside our own agenda in order to walk with a neighbor to help them achieve theirs. These are selfless acts that flow from the heart of a faithful steward and a steward leader. These are not behaviors found on lists of effective management techniques. They are hard to carry out, they take more time and they are difficult to measure. Yet they reflect the ethics of God's kingdom. If we are to serve and manage others from an ethic of love that is lived out through the work of a steward leader it will require us to re-think our management practices, redesign our human resource evaluation processes and retrain our people.

Does it sound impractical? Well, it is if we do it under our own power and attempt to attach secular, common path practices to it. However, if a body of Christ-followers adopts this approach to management as part of a church-wide or ministry-wide commitment to follow the kingdom path we have presented here, we believe it will prove itself to be the most effective and faithful form of encouraging God's people toward fruitfulness.

## Developing a Loving Witness

If we as Christians are to be known for our love, do we work on this at all? Or are we like the religious leaders of the Good Samaritan story who pass by the broken and hurting because we have things to do and places to go? What if coming up with creative ways to show love was a top priority on our daily agenda, weekly church calendar, or monthly ministry outreach? Would it strengthen our witness? Consider three practices for developing a loving witness.

(1) *Personally commit to reflecting on God's love.* This is a divine love dare of sorts. To grow our heart for others, we must allow God to grow our hearts by meditating on His generous love. When we do this, we cannot help but extend love as Teresa of Avila notes:

> May it please His Majesty that the extraordinary generosity He has shown this miserable sinner serve to encourage and rouse those who read this to abandon completely everything for God. If His Majesty repays so fully that even in this life the reward and gain possessed by those who serve Him is clearly seen, what will this reward be in the next life?[33]

How might God stir our hearts through reflecting on His love? Take time over a week or a month for such an exercise with another person or a small group. Share with each other how God worked through the experience. It may be life changing!

(2) *Love often blossoms in community when people serve others together.* Short-term mission trips and service projects are great

examples of this. Such activities help a church family grow spiritually through showing God's love to others as a community. Often we sign up for these events thinking that it's all about the task we are seeking to accomplish, when in reality, the work God does within us through serving is often just as transformational. When we bless others we are equally blessed. Non-participants miss out on the blessing.

(3) *Stop molding and start unfolding.* If we love our neighbor as Christ commands, and if we take a steward leader approach to desiring kingdom outcomes, we will seek to work in concert with the Holy Spirit in helping those around us through a process of unfolding. Think of a flower in spring. The more it unfolds the more beautiful it becomes. That is the joy and privilege we have as Christ-followers who serve others with love. Owner leaders try to mold people into the shape and form that will best serve them, their organization and the results that drive them. Are we molding or unfolding the people around us?

## STEWARDSHIP VIEW OF RESOURCES

The last two marks of Christ-centered ministry deal with our stewardship view of resources. The first one relates to spiritual giftedness. Christ-centered ministry leaders acknowledge that the Holy Spirit is the power of ministry so they help Christ-followers discern their giftedness. This positions the members of Christ's body to use their gifts to bless one another. The second mark tied to a stewardship view of resources encompasses assets, income, and other possessions. Jesus gives stewards explicit instructions on what to do with them, and they are radical compared to the world.

## Mark #9 – Mobilizing Spiritually Gifted People

Near the end of His earthly ministry, Jesus comforted His disciples with the truth that He would send another Comforter that would always be with them (cf. John 14). The Holy Spirit would also serve as Teacher and Guide. Just prior to His ascension into heaven, Jesus adds that the Holy Spirit would empower them to be His witnesses in their city, their nation, and to the ends of the earth (cf. Acts 1:8).

Throughout the book of Acts, the Holy Spirit appears as the main character: guiding, directing, and fueling mission in the early church. God's people do not make ministry happen, the Holy Spirit does. Francis Chan notes: "When believers live in the power of the Spirit, the evidence in their lives is supernatural. The church cannot help but be different, and the world cannot help but notice."[34]

Paul lists gifts of the Spirit and exhorts people to use the gifts they have been given for the common good as members of Christ's body (cf. 1 Corinthians 12; Ephesians 4; Romans 12). Paul also models the path for getting people to participate with God in His work: help them discern their giftedness so they shift from sitting in the stands to getting in the game. In Paul's communications with young leaders like Timothy we learn how to inspire the next generation of leaders to use their gifts. In 2 Timothy 1:6 he writes to Timothy to remind him to "fan into flame the gift of God." Both in the letters to churches and instructions to individuals, Christ-followers are to engage in God's work, empowered by gifts from the Spirit!

*We must remember that people with specific gifts are not to be used like pawns in a chess game.* While it may be common for senior leaders to appoint gifted people for service in specific roles, we must not describe them as assets that we use. Such is the thinking and the language that surfaces from leaders on the common path. Alternatively, on the kingdom path we must celebrate our mutual interdependence rooted in our spiritual gifting. The Body of Christ flourishes only when God's people discern and deploy themselves as God has equipped them.

What are we doing to help God's people discern their gifts? Are we connecting the dots for people between spiritual giftedness and volunteer opportunities? Often we do not mobilize people in service, because we function as though we believe we must pay for God's work to get done. In the early church and for most of church history, volunteers, not paid staff, fueled ministry.

**Helping People Find their Place in the Body of Christ**

Texts such as 1 Peter 4:10 remind us that we are to use the gifts God has given us for the purpose of making known His manifold grace. In other words, people should see Christ through people using their gifts in community. We must not assume people know their giftedness. For assistance in this area, we suggest the following two practices.

(1) *Take a spiritual gifts inventory.* Though you may have done this before, even numerous times, find a fresh one and take it again. You may be surprised. New gifts may be emerging that correspond to your current place of service or ministry. Rather than plow forward, pray about ways to put your gifts to work anew. When you talk about your findings with others, it can both affirm your giftedness and challenge others to discern theirs.

(2) *Offer God's people a spiritual gifts instrument that shows them ways different gifts may be put to work in church or ministry*

*settings.* People find great joy in participating in God's work together, and we must not forget how special it is. Henri Nouwen agrees: "I wonder how many churches and charitable organizations realize that community is one of the greatest gifts they have to offer."³⁵ Do you make it easy for people to use their God-given gifts to work with you in community? If not, start today.

## Mark #10 – Radical Christian Generosity

There is probably no more radical statement about Christian generosity than this one: "For God so loved the world that He gave His one and only Son, that whoever believes in Him shall not perish but have eternal life" (John 3:16). And while all the books in the world could not contain the acts of generosity Christ performed (cf. John 20:30-31), at least three categories come to mind for describing them. With each category we find evidence that the early church also imitated the radical generosity of Jesus.

(1) *Christian generosity is grace-filled not law-based.* When the Word became flesh and dwelled among us, He was full of grace and truth (cf. John 1:14). Since He fulfilled the law for us, when it comes to giving Jesus does not instruct disciples to tithe. Why? That's law language. The only time He speaks of the tithe is when He rebukes the religious leaders for their pride in tithing down to the mint and the spice while failing to exhibit love and justice (cf. Matthew 23:23). Alternatively, He calls His followers to give to God what is God's (cf. Luke 20:25). What is God's? Everything!

Paul states that God wants our hearts and lives as living sacrifices. He reminds us that growth in this area is rooted in grace: "But since you excel in everything—in faith, in speech, in knowledge, in complete earnestness and in the love we have kindled in you—see that you also excel in this grace of giving" (2 Corinthians 8:7). He also urges our motivation to be linked to gratitude. As we are blessed, let us bless others proportionately. We are invited to live this way not because we have to out of compulsion but because we get to out of hearts filled with compassion.

(2) Christian generosity serves the poor rather than showing favoritism to the rich. At the outset of His ministry, Jesus proclaims good news for the poor (cf. Luke 4:18-19). He even touches the destitute viewed culturally as unclean and, in so doing, demonstrates that God's love is for everyone. He invited the poor to follow Him and told the rich to let go of their riches before embarking on the journey.

James speaks pointedly against favoritism in the early church (cf. James 2:1-12). Why? Generosity in the cultural world of the New Testament functioned along the lines of favoritism. People only gave to people who would give them honor, perks, and service in return. Since the poor could offer nothing of value, they were to receive nothing of value. Jesus turns this social norm upside down, or rather, right side up!

(3) *Christian generosity is directed missionally toward people for enjoyment and sharing in community versus amassing earthly property for personal use.* Christ-followers shared resources from a common purse, which they personally supported (John 13:29; Luke 8:3). We have no record that money was spent on anything beyond meeting the needs of people. Though Jesus enjoyed the provision of food and drink, He did not have a place to lay His head during His earthly ministry.

The early church followed suit. They shared everything in common (cf. Acts 2:42–47). They supported those who labor to teach and those who go forth on mission. As a result, no one needed anything among them, including missionaries! Through the rest of the New Testament, the language is linked to having a share in ministry (cf. Galatians 6:6) and participating in the gospel (cf. Philippians 1:3–5). What is most ironic is that we have no record that churches owned facilities. They met in homes. They poured their revenues and treasures into mission and people, not buildings or property.

Why review these three areas in both the Gospels and the early church? They point us to our stewardship, for which we will all be required to give an account (cf. Luke 16:1–9). Charles Hale spoke of the heavenly implications associated with our stewardship. Failure in this area could even adversely influence our eternal destiny (cf. Luke 16:1-9):

The demand of the text will soon be made to each of us: "Give an account of thy stewardship; for thou mayest be no longer steward." Let us conceive the question put to each of us now, could we give our account with joy? Or would it not be given in the case of very many of us, with deepest shame and grief? The talents for which we must give account are the opportunities of all kinds for honoring God and doing good to our fellow men. But, as a searching inquiry is best conducted by coming down from generalities to particulars, let us on the present occasion—putting aside for the time being the thought of health, strength, influence, mental abilities—ask ourselves how we have used, how we are using, the earthly possessions God has put into our hands. The question is more important than we are apt to think. It is our Savior Himself who asks, "If ye have not been faithful in the unrighteous mammon, who will commit to your trust the true riches?" The gift of God cannot be purchased with money, but money not rightly used may cause us to miss heaven.[36]

Other shocking statements surface elsewhere in the New Testament. Christians learned that the purpose of work is not merely to care for the needs of family members but to have something to share with others, and failure to share the fruit of one's labor is depicted as stealing (cf. Ephesians 4:28), just as failing to pay tithes in the Old Testament was robbing God (cf. Malachi 3:8–12). Numerous early church leaders echoed this view. People with the love of God in them share with people in need (cf. 1 John 3:17). As God blesses people, they are to enjoy and share His rich blessings, and these instructions come not as a suggestion but as a command (cf. 1 Timothy 6:17–19).

What is the reward for the obedient rich who enjoy and share all God richly provides? They realize that the life they had linked to money is nothing in comparison to life in God. As Jesus said to the rich man, it's one hundred times better (cf. Mark 10:17–31).

Are we encouraging people to give only a percentage of their time or resources, or are we rallying them to participate with God in His work with all they are and all they have? Are we using law terminology or grace language related to giving?

Do our ministries serve the poor or exhibit favoritism? Are we rallying people to give missionally for enjoyment and sharing? Or does it seem like we want them to pour money into facilities and other property acquisitions? Does it matter?

One pastor functioning from the common path expressed that rather than focus on sowing biblical principles regarding generosity, he just wanted to know what resource he could give them to cause giving to go up five percent so that they could have the funds to pay off a bond on a building. Should that be our focus? Or should pastors teach people stewardship principles so that obedient generosity that reflects the instructions of Jesus springs forth from their lives and so they are prepared to give an account for their stewardship?

### Preparing to Hear the Words "Well Done!"

On this last point linked to the stewardship of material and financial resources, a lot is at stake. Life and eternity are literally up for grabs. We are not saying you can earn your salvation with the path you choose. We are saying that living for money can cause you to miss heaven altogether because Jesus says you cannot serve both God and money.

The question is this: Will you take hold of life and help others do the same? We offer three thoughts for growing in this area and helping others take hold of life that is truly life (cf. 1 Timothy 6:19)!

(1) *The Gospel, not modern opinions, must guide our stewardship and generosity discussions.* David Platt astutely noted:

> We desperately need to explore how much of our understanding of the gospel is American and how much is biblical. And in the process we need to examine whether we have misconstrued a proper response to the gospel and maybe we have missed the primary reward of the gospel, which is God Himself.[37]

This is at the heart of our message in this book. Any assessment of behavior must be evaluated alongside Scripture, not social norms. Just because Christians behave a certain way does not make it right or wrong, especially when the only person to whom every believer will answer someday is Jesus Christ. Our plea is that we live in such a way as to hear Him say to us, "Well done." If a return to the Scriptures as our filter for life and leadership moves people to repentance, revival, and another Great Awakening, then God be praised.

(2) *Personal growth can only take place by evaluating our financial and spiritual house and seeing what needs to be put in order.* Are we putting God's resources to work? Are we storing them up on earth or in heaven? Or are we trying to do both when Jesus specifically says not to? Do our expenses show that we are advancing the gospel and taking care of the poor? Are we living within our means so that we have something to share with others in need or are we slaves to debt because somewhere along the way we bought the line that life was found in having possessions? Putting our house in order is the critical first step to helping others.

(3) *After using the gospel as our guide for conversations, and getting our house in order, let us evaluate our ministry financial statements.* Examine where cash is coming from and where it is going. Do our ministries receive support from most of our families or just a few? In other words, are we raising up givers? Are we investing in buildings or in building up disciples? Do our financials reflect care for the poor? Are we allocating resources to mission? Are we paying our leaders a fair wage (cf. 1 Timothy 5:18)? How much of our revenue goes toward debt, and are we slaves to overspending? Are we pouring money into stuff that has no eternal value and that is not necessary to accomplishing mission? Talk about these areas as a leadership team. Chart a course for change in any areas that do not align with the teaching of Jesus.

## SUMMARY: TEN MARKS

The goal of this chapter was to map a path on which to follow Christ and take good notes. In so doing, ten traits came into view. They comprise the course the first disciples took and mark the kingdom path for us to follow obediently today. We must submit to the Father, while being filled, led, and empowered by the Spirit. That's our operating system. We cannot function any other way as steward leaders!

So that we stay on track, we employ faithfulness-focused strategies related to prayerful strategic planning and raising kingdom resources. Again, we can think of these as the apps we run perpetually. Next, we utilize eternity-oriented metrics that are specifically linked to ministry accountability and transparent financial administration. We do this to exhibit integrity before God and man.

Our posture for management is not driven by results but by nurturing relationships. Our goal is to follow the example of Christ and serve people humbly while doing everything with love. Lastly, aligned with a stewardship view of resources, we seek to mobilize spiritually gifted people. We want to help God's people find a place in kingdom ministry that matches the gifts God has given them. We also exhort everyone to demonstrate radical Christian generosity.

As leaders we must model the way of obedience. We do this by putting all we are and all we have to work in order to make known the gospel.

## CONCLUSION: MAKE THE CHOICE!

Our aim in this book has been to help you redefine success, to prepare you to respond to the three temptations of the devil, and to map the path for the Christ-centered pursuit of kingdom outcomes. The choice to follow the common path or the kingdom path is yours to make. Because we pray this book will spark a revival, we conclude with the inspiring words of Jonathan Edwards:

> We should travel on in a way of obedience to all God's commands, even the difficult as well as the easy commands. We should travel on in a way of self-denial; denying all our sinful inclinations and interests. The way to heaven is ascending; we must be content to travel up hill, though it be hard and tiresome, though it be contrary to the natural tendency and bias of our flesh that tends downward to the earth. We should follow Christ in the path that He has gone in. The way that He travelled in was the right way to heaven. We should take up our cross and follow Him.[38]

## Chapter Seven

# Study Guide and Practical Resources for Pursuing Kingdom Outcomes

*The greatest issue facing the world today, with all its heartbreaking needs, is whether those who, by profession or culture, are identified as "Christians" will become disciples—students, apprentices, practitioners—of Jesus Christ, steadily learning from Him how to live the life of the Kingdom of the Heavens into every corner of human existence. Will they break out of the churches to be His Church—to be, without human force or violence, His mighty force for good on earth, drawing the churches after them toward the eternal purposes of God? And, on its own scale, there is no greater issue facing the individual human being, Christian or not.*[39] Dallas Willard

We don't want readers to come to the end of this book and not have tools for taking action and for rallying others to join them. For this reason, we have included a study guide as well as five practical resources for pursuing kingdom outcomes.

We pray church leadership teams, elder boards, and small groups will read this book and make the choice. We hope ministry governing boards, executives, and employees will do the same! And, as a result, we envision the power being restored to God's Church, like turning on the light in the dark church in Van Gogh's *Starry Night* on this book's cover. This can happen as the Body of Christ together chooses the kingdom path.

## STUDY GUIDE FOR MAKING THE CHOICE TO TAKE THE KINGDOM PATH!

This study guide is intended to help readers process the content and questions contained in each chapter both individually or in group settings. We encourage you to read each chapter, explore the questions for discussion, meditate on related Scriptures, and pray about how God's Spirit may be leading you to respond to the content. And so that we are not simply hearers of God's Word, but so that we do what it says, each section calls you to act, that is, determine to respond in obedience.

### Chapter One

**Read:** Chapter One: How Do We Define and Measure Success?

**Explore:** Questions for Discussion

1. What was your reaction to the opening quote by Thérèse de Lisieux?

2. Have you ever defined success in terms of results and measured it in terms of people, money, or facilities? What did this look like in your life, your church, or other ministry setting?

3. When you hear the term "production-driven leadership" what comes to mind?

4. Have you ever implemented an expansion-focused strategy evaluated by earthly oriented metrics?

5. How are people and resources handled under results-based management and a utilitarian view of resources?

6. What was your reaction to the comment by Phil Vischer? What would it look like for you to cease pursuing impact and instead pursue God?

7. Can you think of a person who exhibits steward leadership? Use words to describe that person.

8. What might a faithfulness-focused strategy evaluated by eternity-oriented metrics look like where you serve? And what qualitative measures could be implemented to ensure things stay on track?

9. What was your reaction to the challenging quote by Chuck Colson on the significance of making choices?

10. Why is it important for Christ-followers to choose the kingdom path rather than the common path?

**Meditate:** Reflect on related Scriptures, 1 Corinthians 4:1-2; John 5:19, 14:10, 15:4; Matthew 28:19-20; John 13:35; 2 Timothy 1:6.

**Pray:** How is the Holy Spirit leading you?

**Act:** What does obedience look like? How will you define and measure success moving forward?

## Chapter Two

**Read:** Chapter Two: The Lies of the Enemy: Three Temptations We All Face

**Explore:** Questions for Discussion

1. What was your reaction to the opening quote by C. S. Lewis?

2. What are you aiming at? In other words, what are you focusing all your energies on?

3. When you read about control, what comes to mind, and why do you think we are so allured by it?

4. What's the opposite of being in or taking control?

5. It is said that anything you feel like you can't live without is an idol. When you read about idolatry, your mind may be drawn to gods made of wood or stone, but what are idols in the modern world?

6. How has mammon become an idol for ministry?

7. What was your reaction to the quote by Philo, a contemporary of Jesus? Does that description make you think of ministry leaders today? In what way?

8. When you read about pride, what comes to mind, and how are Christ-followers tempted in this way?

9. We were made by God to be loved, accepted, and valued. Apart from God, where do people seek love, acceptance, and value?

10. Why is it significant that Jesus faced and overcame these temptations prior to His earthly ministry?

**Meditate:** Reflect on related Scriptures, 1 John 2:15–17; Numbers 20:1–13; Genesis 16; Matthew 14:13–21; 1 Timothy 3:3, 6:10; Matthew 4:1–11.

**Pray:** How is the Holy Spirit leading you?

**Act:** What does obedience look like? How will you respond to the lies of the enemy?

## Chapter Three

**Read:** Chapter Three: Stones to Bread: The Temptation of Control

**Explore:** Questions for Discussion

1. What do you think is the significance of the location of the "stones to bread" temptation?

2. Jesus had the power and the need to make the miracle happen. He was hungry. What was at stake had He succumbed to this temptation?

3. Do we thrive best when we are in control of our lives and destiny?

4. What was your reaction to the related quotes by Andrew Murray and Brother Lawrence?

5. If the enemy attacks where we are weak and vulnerable, in the little things, what are those areas in our lives today?

6. Can you name an area in your life and/or leadership where you could take control if you wanted to, but you must resist this urge?

7. The evil one wants us to focus on the immediate rather than the bigger picture. What are the implications of this?

8. Can you describe an area where the drive for delivering results has led you or someone you know to be tempted to do the expedient rather than the obedient?

9. What changes would need to be made for you to relinquish control in strategic planning related to work or in planning for the future in your personal life?

10. What was your reaction to the closing quote by Henry Blackaby, and how does it relate to your life?

**Meditate:** Reflect on related Scriptures, Luke 4:1–4; Deuteronomy 8; Matthew 4:4; 1 Samuel 13:1–15; 1 Corinthians 2:1–5; 1 Peter 5:5–11; John 15:5.

**Pray:** How is the Holy Spirit leading you?

**Act:** What does obedience look like? How will you resist the temptation of control?

## Chapter Four

**Read:** Chapter Four: All This I Will Give You: The Temptation of Idolatry

**Explore:** Questions for Discussion

1. What do you think is the significance of the location of the "all this I will give you" temptation?

2. What do our high places look like today? In other words, have we been trustworthy to put God's resources to work or have we set up financial safety nets in case God's plan for us differs from our own?

3. If we are slaves to whatever we think we own, to what kinds of things are we enslaved today?

4. Do you believe money is needed for ministry to happen? If not, then what is the one thing required for ministry to happen?

5. What can we do to be sure we are not serving mammon and acting as lovers of money like the religious leaders did in the time of Jesus?

6. What takes place today when we commit the sin described by Tozer as the "monstrous substitution"?

7. If rejecting idols is about letting go of false things so we can take hold of what it true, how have we in our personal lives and in ministry settings committed the sin of idolatry when we talk about financial sustainability?

8. How does God want our lives and ministries sustained?

9. Hatmaker testified that "in the quantity of ordinary obedience" the kingdom advances. Can you name the kinds of behaviors that this might refer to in a person's life and in ministry settings?

10. What is your reaction to the closing quote by St. Augustine?

**Meditate:** Reflect on related Scriptures, Luke 4:5–8, 16:10–15; Mark 12:38–40; Deuteronomy 6; 2 Corinthians 8:21; Matthew 6:32, 7:7–11.

**Pray:** How is the Holy Spirit leading you?

**Act:** What does obedience look like? How will you resist the temptation of idolatry?

## Chapter Five

**Read:** Chapter Five: Leap of Fame: The Temptation of Pride

**Explore:** Questions for Discussion

1. What do you think is the significance of the location of the "leap of fame" temptation, especially related to the launching of the earthly ministry of Jesus?

2. Satan manipulated Scripture with this temptation. How have we been guilty of that and how can we avoid it?

3. Can we be popular, even famous, and do great things but totally miss participating with God in His work? What examples come to mind as you answer this question?

4. If our actions reveal our heart condition, what kinds of actions communicate that there is pride in our hearts?

5. To avoid the damaging effects of pride, how can we see every decision as an opportunity to discern God's agenda for the church or ministry we serve? In other words, what changes do we need to make for this to be true?

6. How does pride surface in our personal or professional decision-making?

7. What is your reaction to the Hudson Taylor quote?

8. Could our prideful self-perception be our greatest limiting factor? How are we our own worst enemies?

9. How do our busy schedules reflect pride and the desire for the applause of others?

10. What are ways we can rest in God despite the busy pace of the world in which we live?

**Meditate:** Reflect on related Scriptures, Luke 4:9–13; Exodus 17; Philippians 2:1–11; Acts 16:7–8; Matthew 11:28–30; Mark 6:31; James 4:4–10.

**Pray:** How is the Holy Spirit leading you?

**Act:** What does obedience look like? How will you resist the temptation of pride and the allure of approval?

## Chapter Six

**Read:** Chapter Six: Following Christ: Ten Marks of Christ-Centered Ministry

**Explore:** Questions for Discussion

1. What is your reaction to the George Mueller quote that opened the chapter?

2. What does it mean that these ten marks are formational and not formulaic, and that they are descriptive rather than prescriptive?

3. Summarize "submission to the Father" and what it means to be "filled, led, and empowered by the Holy Spirit" in your own words. Describe a practice that you desire to apply to grow in this aspect of steward leadership.

4. The faithfulness-focused strategies of prayerful strategic planning and raising kingdom resources are intended to keep

us in a posture of dependence. Describe why this is important and what happens when we are not in this place.

5. The kingdom path calls for the eternity-oriented metrics of ministry accountability and transparent financial administration. What are the risks of having the wrong metrics, inadequate ministry accountability, and lack of transparency linked to finances?

6. When management is based on relationships rather than results, how does this impact the productivity of staff?

7. When ministry exhibits love and service, how would that shape the world's perception of Christians?

8. What are your spiritual gifts, and how are you putting them to work in service to others for God's glory?

9. What resources in your possession are not being handled consistent with the instructions of Jesus?

10. Are you raising up gifts for your ministry or raising up givers for God's kingdom? What's the difference?

**Meditate:** Reflect on related Scriptures, John 15:19–30; Acts 6:4; Galatians 5:22–23; Acts 15; Luke 6:12–13; Acts 13:1–3; Luke 9:1–6, 10:1–24, 22:35–38; Acts 4:36–37; 1 Timothy 3:1–13, 2 Corinthians 8:20–21; Luke 22:24–27; 1 Peter 5:3; Mark 12:30–31; Galatians 6:10–11; 1 Peter 4:10; Luke 20:25; 1 Timothy 6:17–19.

**Pray:** How is the Holy Spirit leading you?

**Act:** What does obedience look like? Can you choose at least one formational practice to adopt in your life?

## RESOURCES FOR MAKING THE CHOICE
## TO FOLLOW THE KINGDOM PATH

### Resource #1: The Seven Marks of the Steward Leader

We have used the term steward leader throughout this book. The following table sums up what we believe are the seven marks of a steward leader in seven statements that are rooted in biblical truth. We offer this list for you and your board or leadership team as you talk about steward leadership. Since these statements are brief, there are numerous ways they can be put forth for discussion. We suggest three:

(1) *Self-reflection.* Take a week and reflect on one statement per day. What does it look like in your own life? Journal your thoughts. How is it linked to your leadership? Again, journal some more. Ask the Holy Spirit to show you areas where you have room for growth.

(2) *Board or staff meeting dialogue.* Print these seven marks on one page and distribute them. Divide people in seven groups, or if your numbers are small, have each person take one of the marks. Each person or group reads the mark, summarizes it in their own words, and says why it is important to believe and act on that statement.

(3) *Seven short discussions.* If your leadership team meets often, consider discussing one mark at each meeting for seven meetings. Again, be sure to give everyone a chance to share. Take time to pray for one another that each mark may be evident in each person's life.

| | The Seven Marks of a Steward Leader |
|---|---|
| 1. | Steward leaders *understand that their lives are not their own.* They are stewards of every area of life and resist the temptation to play the role of master. They daily take a posture of listening for God's leading and responding with joyful obedience. |
| 2. | Steward leaders *seek intimacy with God as their highest calling.* They prioritize activities that nurture this intimacy and reject the temptation to allow urgent matters to rob them of it. They follow God's leading wherever it may take them and the ministry. |
| 3. | Steward leaders *are secure in their identities in Jesus Christ.* They stand firm on that certainty and reject the temptation to desire affirmation or applause from any other source. This positions them to absorb criticism and deflect praise. |
| 4. | Steward leaders *see those with whom they lead and serve as fellow pilgrims.* They shun the temptation to use others to further their own agendas. Consequently, they encourage the personal and spiritual growth of those they lead and with whom they serve. |
| 5. | Steward leaders *regard all resources as gifts from God.* They resist the temptation to hoard or waste them. Instead, they put them to work consistent with instructions in God's Word and the leading of the Holy Spirit, and they do this for God's glory. |
| 6. | Steward leaders *recognize the spiritual battle they are in as they strive to lead as faithful stewards in a world of people playing the role of master.* They speak the truth, which sets people free from bondage so they may experience abundant life. |
| 7. | Steward leaders *have learned that victory starts with surrender.* They set aside the temptation to self-reliance and take on the mantle of a leader of no reputation. Only after abandoning everything can a steward effectively lead. |

## Resource #2: The Roadmap for Pursuing Kingdom Outcomes

We realize that after reading this book you need something in your hands, a roadmap of sorts, to facilitate a discussion with your board, leadership team, and other co-laborers in the kingdom. This roadmap has three parts. For example, at a board retreat, the first part could be done in one evening, and the second and third parts could be tackled the following morning.

### Part One: Two Paths

| The Common Path | The Kingdom Path |
|---|---|
| Production-Driven Leadership | Steward Leadership |
| Expansion-Focused Strategies | Faithfulness-Focused Strategies |
| Earthly Oriented Metrics | Eternity-Oriented Metrics |
| Results-Based Management | Relationship-Based Management |
| Utilitarian View of Resources | Stewardship View of Resources |

How do the practices at our churches or organizations reveal how we define success? Senior leaders must take time to think about how their leadership is shaping either a culture chasing results or a culture pursuing obedience. We can also take time to discuss these items openly together. We suggest allowing at least ninety minutes for this seven-step group exercise.

(1) *Call for prayer.* Before initiating a conversation on this topic, we suggest calling the board or leadership team together and, in advance, ask them to pray for wisdom and insight from the Lord regarding what success looks like.

(2) *Read aloud the ten descriptions.* When you come together, have people take turns reading the brief descriptions that define the five characteristics of both the common path and the kingdom path.

(3) *Divide people into five groups.* If your numbers are small, then perhaps do the remaining steps as a large group. The goal here is that everyone participates in the conversation.

(4) *Get people talking.* Assign the five pairs of characteristics to the five groups and ask each of them to discuss how both the common path and kingdom path characteristics appear at the church or ministry.

(5) *Share ideas.* Invite each group to share ways that the ministry can stay on the kingdom path with respect to each characteristic.

(6) *Discuss next steps.* If it is a board meeting, the chair may suggest asking the leadership to review policies that need to be revised. If it is a staff meeting, the team may evaluate policies and procedures by area of responsibility.

(7) *Make the choice.* We are not suggesting that leaders decide all the changes they want to make in one meeting. By calling leaders to make the choice, we are simply suggesting that leaders make the choice to change paths as necessary in order to pursue kingdom outcomes.

## Part Two: Three Temptations: Control, Idolatry and Pride

| Three Temptations: Control, Idolatry, and Pride | | |
|---|---|---|
| **Deception #1** | **Deception #2** | **Deception #3** |
| "the Lust of the Flesh" | "the Lust of the Eyes" | "the Pride of Life" |
| Who's in control? | Whom do we serve? | In whom will we base our identity? |

This next part may be best done in a devotional manner reflecting on Luke 4:1–13. Again, there are many ways you could do this as an individual, with a leadership team, or in a board meeting setting. This can be done in thirty to sixty minutes.

Start with prayer asking the Spirit to teach and guide each person. Whether as an individual or in a group setting, read Luke 4:1–13 aloud. Sit in silence. Read it aloud again and stop after each temptation. Ask participants to sit quietly with the Lord and consider how each temptation appears personally.

Give them margin to journal biblical truths that come to mind linked to each temptation. Challenge each person to resolve to resist these temptations, standing firm in the faith. Close your time with prayer.

## Part Three: Ten Marks of Christ-Centered Ministry

| Following Christ: Ten Marks of Christ-Centered Ministry | |
|---|---|
| Steward Leadership | (1) Submission to the Father<br>(2) Filled, Led and Empowered by the Holy Spirit |
| Faithfulness-Focused Strategies | (3) Prayerful Strategic Planning<br>(4) Raising Kingdom Resources |
| Eternity-Oriented Metrics | (5) Ministry Accountability<br>(6) Transparent Financial Administration |
| Relationship-Based Management | (7) Serving People Humbly<br>(8) Doing Everything with Love |
| Stewardship View of Resources | (9) Mobilizing Spiritually Gifted People<br>(10) Radical Christian Generosity |

Our target for this third part is about three hours with a break in the middle. This means that you have about fifteen minutes to discuss each point. Try to cover five marks in seventy-five minutes and then break. Cover the other five after your break. As the facilitator, your objective is to get people talking and interacting with these marks. We suggest you don't approach each of the ten areas the same but mix things up to keep your group engaged.

For example, ask groups to help define these marks. Groups can share what they believe submission to the Father looks like in a person's life and leadership. Another way to approach these is to share one or more of the Scripture verses linked to each one and talk about how the groups see that mark in God's Word and how they see it at the ministry or church.

So that participants do not disconnect this from the organization, perhaps with each mark, ask staff to comment on what policies and/or procedures may be linked to those marks. This process will bring to light areas for growth. As such, it may be good to do this exercise annually, such as when new board members or leadership team members are oriented. The ultimate goal in going through these ten marks together is to build ownership and community consensus around the choice to take the kingdom path.

### Resource #3: The Commitments of the Christ-Centered Ministry

One result that can come from having facilitated discussions around the topic of pursuing the kingdom path is an official organizational statement. Such statements can help reshape the culture of a ministry, especially if it has been on the common path. To follow is a sample document that you may choose to adopt or adapt.

As God's people, called together for the purpose of the mission of this ministry, we commit:

(1) To understand the teachings of Jesus and obey them regardless of the implications in our culture or within the organization.

(2) To listen intently as a community for the leading of the Holy Spirit and affirm together the vision for our ministry that arises from what we have heard.

(3) To be obedient to the Spirit's leading and pursue that vision without hesitation or fear, trusting God to be our Sustainer and Provider.

(4) To align our systems, policies, and practices to the vision regardless of the cost.

(5) To measure our success solely in terms of our faithfulness in advancing that vision.

(6) To develop our plans and create our strategies focused on the work God calls us to accomplish to achieve that vision.

(7) To lead our people in the fullest use of their skills and spiritual giftedness, connecting every action to the fulfillment of that vision.

(8) To invest God's resources entrusted to us to pursue that vision with passion and joy.

(9) To measure all of our work in kingdom terms and undertake all of our work under the sole guidance of kingdom values.

(10) To surrender our desire for control, denounce the love of money, shun worldly praise, and take up the mantel of Christ-centered ministry to the glory of God.

As a leadership team, we annually affirm these commitments to maintain our Christ-centeredness in pursuit of kingdom outcomes.

## Resource #4: The Choice: Rule of Life

Only after people have studied the content of this book do we want them to consider this offer. We invite you to adopt the Rule of Life on the next page. Read through it.

So what do you think? Are you in? If so, find a friend to witness your decision. Perhaps invite them to join you. We pray that by calling people to this Rule of Life that the Spirit will catalyze a movement of disciples determined to follow the kingdom path.

## The Choice: Rule of Life

As a follower of Jesus Christ, I commit:

1. To define success as obedience to the teachings of Jesus Christ in God's Word

2. To resist the temptation of control by instead placing my confidence in God's promises

3. To resist the temptation of idolatry and trusting in money or possessions rather than God

4. To resist the temptation of pride by finding my identity and affirmation in Christ alone

5. To submit to the Father and be filled, led, and empowered by the Holy Spirit

6. To employ faithfulness-focused strategies related to prayerful strategic planning and raising kingdom resources

7. To utilize eternity-oriented metrics for ministry accountability and transparent financial administration

8. To manage relationships rather than results from a posture of humility and doing everything with love

9. To mobilize spiritually gifted people and exhort them to demonstrate radical Christian generosity

10. To model steward leadership that glorifies God and points the way so that others may follow

I adopt this rule of life in the presence of this witness with one goal, that I might run with perseverance the race marked out for me, and someday hear two words from our Lord Jesus Christ: "Well done!"

Signature: _____

Witness: _____ Date _____

## Resource #5: The Choice Book Website

Take a moment to visit www.thechoicebook.org. There you will find additional resources to assist you in your journey. Making the choice is only the first step. The content on this website is intended to help you stay on track and finish well.

# Endnotes

[1] David Platt, *Radical Together: Unleashing the People of God for the Purpose of God* (Colorado Springs: Multnomah, 2011) 3.

[2] Thérèse de Lisieux, as recounted in *The Confirmed Catholic's Companion: A Guide to Abundant Living*, ed. M. K. Glavich (Chicago: ACTA Publications, 2005) 71.

[3] Phil Vischer as quoted by Megan Basham, "It's Not About the Dream," *World*, September 24, 2011, accessed December 5, 2013, http://www.worldmag.com/2011/09/it_s_not_about_the_dream.

[4] John Calvin, *Institutes of the Christian Religions* (Edinburgh: T&T Clark, 1863) 3.7.2.

[5] Charles Colson, *Loving God* (Grand Rapids: Zondervan, 1996) 92.

[6] C. S. Lewis, *Mere Christianity* (New York: Harper Collins, 2001) 134.

[7] Andrew Murray, *Waiting on God* (Renaissance Classics, 2012) 7.

[8] Brother Lawrence, *The Practice of the Presence of God: The Best Rule of a Holy Life* (New York: Fleming H. Revell, 1895) 27.

[9] For further reading on this subject, see: Ruth Haley Barton, *Pursuing God's Will Together: A Discernment Practice for Leadership Groups* (Downers Grove: IVP, 2012); Ruth Haley Barton, *Strengthening the*

*Soul of Your Leadership: Seeking God in the Crucible of Ministry* (Downers Grove: IVP, 2008); and Ruth Haley Barton, *Sacred Rhythms: Arranging our Lives for Spiritual Transformation* (Downers Grove: IVP, 2006).

[10] Henry Blackaby, *Experiencing God: Knowing and Doing the Will of God*, rev. and exp. (Nashville: B & H Publishing, 2008) 233.

[11] A. W. Tozer, *The Pursuit of God* (Camp Hill: Christian Publications, 1982) 22.

[12] A. W. Tozer, *The Root of the Righteous* (Harrisburg: Christian Publications, 1955) 50.

[13] For further reading on this topic, see: Scott Rodin's monograph on endowment keeping, R. Scott Rodin, *Toward a Theology of Endowment Keeping* (Winchester: ECFA, 2010).

[14] Jen Hatmaker, *Seven: Clothes, Spending, Waste, Stress, Media, Possessions, Food—An Experimental Mutiny Against Excess* (Nashville: B&H Publishing, 2012) 114.

[15] St. Augustine, Bishop of Hippo, *Letter* 203.

[16] Hudson Taylor, as recounted in Daniel Whyte III (Dallas: Torch Legacy, 2010) 91.

[17] George Mueller, as cited by Stephen A. Macchia, *Crafting a Rule of Life: An Invitation to the Well-Ordered Way* (Downers Grove: IVP, 2012) 121–22.

[18] Mother Teresa, *Come Be My Light*, ed. Brian Kolodiejchuk (New York: Doubleday, 2007) 87.

19 "Jonathan Edwards Resolutions." Accessed on December 6, 2013, http://www.apuritansmind.com/the-christian-walk/jonathan-edwards-resolutions/. See also: Daniel Whyte III, *How to Forget the Troubles, Problems, and Failures of the Past and Make this the Best Year of Your Life* (Dallas: Torch Legacy, 2011) 53.

20 Dietrich Bonhoeffer, *The Cost of Discipleship* (New York: SCM Press, 1959) 11.

21 John Milton, as recounted in *The Westminster Collection of Christian Quotations*, comp. Martin H. Mansur (Louisville: Westminster John Knox Press, 2001) 87.

22 John Chrysostom, *Homilies on Romans 9*.

23 Severian of Gabala, *Catena*. CEC 29.

24 John MacArthur, *Found: God's Will* (Colorado Springs: David C. Cook, 2012) 67.

25 In *Celebration of Discipline: The Path to Spiritual Growth*, Richard Foster noted four inward disciplines: prayer, study, fasting, and meditation. With the first mark, we spoke of the importance of prayer and study. Here we are calling for the other two: meditation and fasting.

26 Jenni Hoag, personal communication, September 12, 2013.

27 Jonathan Goforth, as recounted by his wife, Rosalind Goforth, *Climbing: Memories of a Missionary's Wife* (Grand Rapids: Zondervan, 1940) 197.

[28] Adoniram Judson, *The American Baptist Magazine and Missionary Intelligencer*, vol. 1. (Boston: James Loring and Lincoln & Edmands, 1817) 99.

[29] For further discussion on this topic, see: R. Scott Rodin and Gary G. Hoag, *The Sower: Redefining the Ministry of Raising Kingdom Resources* (Winchester: ECFA Press, 2010).

[30] Need assistance? Pick up a copy of *Crafting a Rule of Life: An Invitation to the Well-Ordered Way* by Stephen A Macchia. As you will see in chapter seven, our hope is that you will adopt the path outlined in this book as a rule of life.

[31] Henri J. M. Nouwen, *The Spirituality of Fundraising* (Richmond Hill: Estate of Henri J. M. Nouwen, 2004) 6.

[32] John Wesley, *The Works of Rev. John Wesley, A.M.*, vol. 13 (London: Wesleyan Conference Office, 1872) 9.

[33] Teresa of Avila, *The Book of Her Life*, trans, with notes by Kieran Kavanaugh, O.C.D. and Otilio Rodrigueq, O.C.D. (Indianapolis: Hackett, 2008) 138.

[34] Francis Chan, *Forgotten God: Reversing Our Tragic Neglect of the Holy Spirit* (Colorado Springs: David C. Cook, 2009) 17.

[35] Henri J. M. Nouwen, *The Spirituality of Fundraising* (Richmond Hill: Estate of Henri J. M. Nouwen, 2004) 28.

[36] Rev. Charles R. Hale, "Give an Account of Thy Stewardship," a sermon preached in St. Timothy's Church, New York, on the third Sunday of Advent, 1873. Accessed December 6, 2013 at http://anglicanhistory.org/usa/crhale/stewardship.html

[37] David Platt, *Radical: Taking Back Your Faith from the American Dream* (Colorado Springs: Multnomah, 2010), 28, italics added.

[38] Jonathan Edwards, *The Works of President Edwards*, vol. 4 (New York: Leavitt & Allen, 1852) 575.

[39] Dallas Willard, *The Great Omission: Reclaiming Jesus's Essential Teachings on Discipleship* (New York: HarperCollins, 2006) xv.

# The Authors

**Gary G. Hoag,** Ph.D., has dedicated his life to encouraging Christian generosity as the Generosity Monk. He provides spiritual and strategic counsel for denominational leaders on nurturing a culture of generosity in local church settings and helps ministry leaders rally God's people to participate with them in God's work. He formerly served as vice president of advancement at Denver Seminary and Colorado Christian University. He currently lectures and teaches at seminaries around the world. He coauthored *The Sower: Redefining the Ministry of Raising Kingdom Resources*, served as a content reviewer for the *NIV Stewardship Study Bible*, and has authored chapters in other books as well as numerous articles. He has also volunteered on the following boards: Association of Theological Schools—Development and Institutional Advancement Professionals (ATS–DIAP), Christian Stewardship Association (CSA), and Christian Leadership Alliance (CLA).

**R. Scott Rodin,** Ph.D., has a passion for helping Christian has a passion for helping Christian ministries take a biblical approach to leadership development, strategic planning, board development, and fundraising. For thirty years he has served as counsel, coach, and trainer to not-for-profit organizations in the United States, Canada, the Middle East, Great Britain, China, the Philippines and Australia. He leads Rodin Consulting Inc. and is past president of the Christian Stewardship Association and of the Eastern Baptist Theological Seminary in Philadelphia. He is a Senior Fellow of the Association of Biblical Higher Education and serves on the boards of ChinaSource and the Evangelical Environmental Network. He coauthored *The Sower: Redefining the Ministry of Raising Kingdom Resources* and has written other ten books including: *The Million-Dollar Dime, The Third Conversion, The Steward Leader, The Seven Deadly Sins of Christian Fundraising*, and *Stewards in the Kingdom*.

**Wesley K. Willmer**, Ph.D., CCNL. Throughout his career of more than four decades, he has initiated and directed more than $1 million in research grants to study faith-based nonprofit management practices, and he is responsible for twenty-four books and many professional journal articles. Besides consulting ( Wes Willmer Group, LLC) with a wide variety of ministries, he has served as a volunteer on numerous boards, including serving for six years as the chair of the Christian Stewardship Association, being a founding board member of the Council for the Advancement and Support of Education's (CASE) Commission on Philanthropy, serving as vice chair of the ECFA (Evangelical Council for Financial Accountability) board, and being a founding board member of the Christian Leadership Alliance (CLA). He can be reached at Wes.Willmer@gmail.com

**The Sower** – by R. Scott Rodin and Gary Hoag

This book is aimed at the heart of every person who is involved in the process of raising money or giving money for the work of God's Kingdom. You may be a full-time development officer, an executive director, a pastor, a president, a board member, a volunteer, or a faithful giver. You may have decades of experience in fund development, or this may be your first exposure to this topic. If you care about giving or raising money for God's work, this book is for you.

**Zondervan Church and Nonprofit Tax & Financial Guide** – by Dan Busby, Michael Martin, and John Van Drunen

This annual reference guide continues to be one of the few resources offering tax and financial advice to churches and nonprofit organizations. Issues of financial accountability, receiving and maintaining tax-exempt status, accounting for charitable gifts, and other crucial topics receive careful and full discussion. This guide is indispensable to church treasurers and anyone else responsible for the financial operation of a nonprofit organization.

**Zondervan Minister's Tax & Financial Guide** – by Dan Busby, Michael Martin, and John Van Drunen

The voluminous laws and regulations that apply to ministers are mind-boggling. This easy-to-understand workbook defies the complexity of the topics covered and offers dozens of tips to reduce the minister's tax bill. The guide includes a line-by-line explanation of the 1040 Form as well as information on recent changes in the tax code.

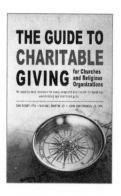

**The Guide To Charitable Giving for Churches and Religious Organizations** – by Dan Busby, Michael Martin, and John Van Drunen

The guide will be your one-stop resource for questions surrounding the proper handling of unrestricted and restricted gifts. This comprehensive, yet easy-to-read guide will contain numerous examples and sample illustrations to help you navigate some of the most common and challenging charitable giving scenarios faced by churches and other religious organizations.

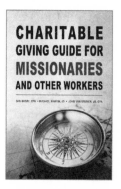

**Charitable Giving Guide for Missionaries and Other Workers** – by Dan Busby, Michael Martin, and John Van Drunen

Many charities, including churches and parachurch organizations, sponsor individuals that serve on domestic and international mission trips. Often missionaries or other workers are responsible for raising gifts to provide support to pay for part or all of the mission trip expenses. This simple, how-to guide includes numerous examples, sample illustrations, and the basic guidelines to follow for handling mission-related gifts.

**Charitable Giving Guide for Short-Term Mission Trips** – by Dan Busby, Michael Martin, and John Van Drunen

The proper handling of funds raised and expended for short-term mission trips often presents challenging tax, finance, and legal issues for trip participants and sending organizations alike. The administration of these trips is an opportunity for churches and other charities to model integrity and compliance with the law. The guide includes numerous examples and sample illustrations.

*Available at ECFAPress • ECFA.org/ECFAPress.aspx*

# More Resources from the Authors

### The Third Conversion – by R. Scott Rodin

*The Third Conversion* is a call to ministry leaders, development professionals, and every ministry supporter who cares about being a steward of what God has given us. Written in an engaging, fictional style, *The Third Conversion* will challenge the conventional way we raise and give money for Christian work. The story of Walt and Carl is a parable of the biblical way of looking at our giving and asking as workers in the kingdom of God.

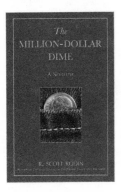

### The Million-Dollar Dime – by R. Scott Rodin

In *The Million-Dollar Dime* the lives of a former drug dealer, a discouraged pastor, a wealthy widow, a defiant stewardship committee chairman, and a ministry development officer intersect on one momentous night where they are changed forever by one small, thin dime. And so will yours, if you are willing to take up the challenge issued by a brave young woman in the face of insurmountable odds—if all you had were God and a dime, you would have enough?

### The Steward Leader – by R. Scott Rodin

This is not a "how-to" book on leadership. It is a "who" book. Its thesis is based on the premise that without a clear understanding and commitment to the "who" of leadership, talking about the "how" will be unfulfilling, impossible to sustain, and ultimately will do a disservice to the Christian leader. The book unpacks the question of who we are as God's stewards—ones to whom have been given the vocation and privilege of stewarding God's gifts given to us at four levels.

*These books are available at kingdomlifepublishing.com*

# More Resources from the Authors

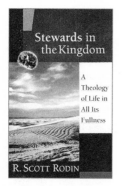

**Stewards in the Kingdom** – by R. Scott Rodin

*Stewards in the Kingdom* provides a full and fresh picture of being Jesus' disciples and living life in all of its fullness. The book unpacks what it means for us to be stewards in the kingdom of the triune God of grace. Rodin dismantles the myth of the two kingdoms, one that is under God's control and one that is not. In doing so, he crafts a portrait of faithful stewards who live as God's children in the reality that is marked by death behind us and life ahead.

**Revolution in Generosity: Transforming Stewards to Be Rich Toward God** –Wesley K. Willmer, editor, with chapters by Gary G. Hoag and R. Scott Rodin

The over 20 authors in this book are proposing that the God-honoring approach of providing resources is to focus on transforming stewards. It is human nature to be like the rich fool in Luke 12:21, who "lays up treasure for himself. The goal of this book is to embrace biblical stewardship and generous giving, thereby encouraging stewards who are rich toward God.

**God & Your Stuff: The Vital Link Between Our Earthly Possession and Eternal Soul** – by Wesley K. Willmer

This book explores the biblical foundation and practical application for the crucial connection between our eternal souls and our earthly possessions. Learn how our use of possessions is a good barometer of our character, and how our giving practices develop our faith and shape us into the stewards God intended us to be.

*Stewards in the Kingdom is available at kingdomlifepublishing.com, and the other two books may be purchased at Amazon.com.*